NOV 22 1952

**WITHDRAWN
NDSU**

EUROPEAN MANIFESTO

BOOKS BY PIERRE DE LANUX

La Yougoslavie, *Paris 1916*
Young France and New America, *New York 1917*
Eveil d'une Ethique Internationale, *Paris 1924*
La Vie de Henry IV, *Paris 1927*
Sud (the American South), *Paris 1932*
La Neutralité Américaine, *Paris 1936*
Render unto Man, *New York 1940*
France de ce Monde, *New York, Editions Françaises 1941*
Têtes de Pont, *New York, Brentano 1942*

European

Manifesto

BY PIERRE DE LANUX

CREATIVE AGE PRESS, INC.
11 East 44th Street, New York, N. Y.

COPYRIGHT 1945 BY PIERRE DE LANUX

ALL RIGHTS IN THIS BOOK ARE RESERVED. NO PART OF THE BOOK MAY BE REPRODUCED IN ANY MANNER WHATSOEVER WITHOUT WRITTEN PERMISSION, EXCEPT IN THE CASE OF BRIEF QUOTATIONS EMBODIED IN CRITICAL ARTICLES AND REVIEWS.

PRINTED IN THE UNITED STATES OF AMERICA
BY AMERICAN BOOK—STRATFORD PRESS, INC., NEW YORK

CONTENTS

THE HARD CORE OF EUROPE 3
TEN NATIONS, 136 MILLION PEOPLE. A SINGLE WAR OF INDEPENDENCE. THE BIRTH OF A GREAT POWER.

THE OTHER COMPONENTS 8
ENGLAND. RUSSIA. THE NEUTRALS. THE FORMER AXIS SATELLITES.

STRUCTURE AND POLICIES 16
FRONTIERS. AIMS OF NATIONAL POLICIES. FORCE. THE PRACTICAL ENFORCEMENT OF ORDER. LEAGUES OLD AND NEW. EUROPEAN ECONOMY. "POPULAR FRONTS." CONVERGENCE OF VALID TRADITIONS. THE SPIRITUAL FUNCTION OF EUROPE.

GERMANY 41
NATURE OF THE GERMANS. THE NEXT WAR. THE EUROPEAN SOLUTION. NATURE OF THE GUILT.

FRANCE 57
FRANCE IN EUROPE. PERSONAL FREEDOM AND NATIONAL UNITY. THE QUEST FOR MAN. FRENCH POLICIES. FROM EMPIRE TO FEDERATION.

REPUBLIC VERSUS EMPIRE 73
"THE GREAT DESIGN." NATIONALISM ALIVE. THE INTERNATIONAL RESPONSIBILITIES OF MAN.

THE AMERICAN ANGLE 90

AMERICA IN THE DISTANCE. AMERICAN LEADERSHIP, PRESENT OR ABSENT. POSITION OF THE U.S. TODAY. U.S. WORLD PLANS. THE U.S. AND THE NEW EUROPE. AMERICA WILL BE PROMISES.

NEW CHARTS 117

MEN AGAINST MAN. BEYOND DEMOCRACY. VOCATION AND FREEDOM. RENDER UNTO MAN. ON THE IMPORTANCE OF SEEING NEW THINGS WITH NEW EYES.

NOTES 133

1. EUROPE: POPULATION FIGURES.
2. THE WAY OF ALL CONQUEST.
3. THE FUTURE THAT WAS.
4. HOW WE FAILED.
5. THE AWAKENING.
6. FROM "NOTES TO MY FRIENDS" (1940–1941).

EUROPEAN MANIFESTO

THE HARD CORE OF EUROPE

TEN NATIONS, 136 MILLION PEOPLE

THE FRENCH UNDERGROUND NEWSPAPER *Combat*, IN ITS 53rd issue December 1943, published a leading article entitled "Our Europe."

The article was written as an answer to a speech by Marshal Smuts, of South Africa, who had minimized the part to be played in the future of Europe by "second-rate" powers, France among them.

Instead of voicing the traditional reaction of offended nationalism, *Combat* stresses France's solidarity with other European nations: "The list is a long one: Czechoslovakia, Poland, Norway, Denmark, Holland, Belgium, Luxembourg, Greece, Yugoslavia . . . the Europe of the Resistance. Here is France's place. Here is her mission. Not in a theoretical Europe that may be cut out by diplomats of the Great Powers, but with this tortured Europe, this underground Europe, which is stricken yet strikes back. Here is our brotherhood. Here is our future.

"We have more in common with a man of the *Libre Belgique* or with one of Tito's men, than with the most pro-French of diplomats. This is the Internationale of the Resistance.

"That is why we are indifferent as to whether we shall be called a Great Power or not. With or without Marshal

Smuts the European resistance is going to re-make Europe. A free Europe of free citizens, because we have known slavery. A united Europe, politically and economically, because we have paid the price for being divided. An armed Europe because we have paid the price for being weak.

"France as the first among the Small Powers, why not? Such a Europe with its overseas possessions would have little cause to envy the British Empire or the Soviet Union, either in population, wealth, or size."

I do not know who wrote this. I hope to meet him some day. Inasmuch as he speaks for the Underground of ten European countries whose total population is 136 million, I consider his text to be of historical importance.

What he says implies:

1. Solidarity among ten nations who have suffered the same fate at the same time and are fighting the same war of independence.

2. Mutual support and a common policy among these ten nations, to avoid piecemeal destruction or absorption, either by invasion or by economic colonization.

3. Confidence in their united strength.

This takes us out of the realm of academic or diplomatic plans and discussions as to what sort of Europe might be desirable in a more or less distant future.

It confronts us with the Europe that is.

A SINGLE WAR OF INDEPENDENCE

This is not a thing on paper, or a move in a game. It is taking place in people's hearts and entrails. It is the birth of a creature alive.

THE HARD CORE OF EUROPE

For the first time, we find that intense patriotism has led whole populations to determined internationalism.

Whereas it has been taken for granted that inspiration and leadership would come to Europe from outside, and that the people downtrodden and hunted by Nazis and their servants would emerge with just enough energy to survive, it seems that these people have done more thinking than we have. They have made up their minds about problems which we still regard as lying ahead of us.

I am not basing my conclusions on a single text. I have had many conversations with men who have come directly from inside Europe; I have listened to leaders, heard news from the occupied countries, and read many documents from their uncensored papers. They all agree.

The old Europe is gone. The Europe of many unrelated and rival "sovereign" units could not last, and Hitler has proved it by destroying it piecemeal.

Hitler's Europe is gone too. Its monstrous existence could not last, and the Germans themselves have murdered the German dream of a huge disciplined empire under Teutonic masters.

The Third Europe has been born through insurrection, as most countries have been born. We had thought about it. We had planned it before it was ready. The insurgents have made it.

Their decision to hang together so as not to hang separately, resembles strangely the decision of the American colonies, to unite for the common defense of their freedom and the pursuit of happiness. Americans should be the last to express surprise at what is happening. They should recognize it as familiar.

THE BIRTH OF A GREAT POWER

These ten nations are the hard core, the backbone of a new Europe. Their people are 136 million on the Continent with another 143 million associated with them or under their direct control overseas—French, Dutch and Belgian commonwealths of colonies, protectorates or mandates.

Europe, the whole of it, rests on a firm triangle: this federation of ten, England and Russia.

The relations of this initial federation of ten to the remaining European nations will be examined in the following chapters. It is too soon to know whether the neutrals of today, the present satellites of Germany, and ultimately Germany herself, will be added to this nucleus. This European federation will undoubtedly be the solution for some, but others will steer closer to England or Russia. Reasons of interest will decide. We may expect to see overlapping, interlocking spheres of influence between great powers rather than any strict delimitation that would hold a nation wholly within the shadow of a single ally or protector. Some small nations are likely to fluctuate between various influences. But for reasons of protection, of trade and of culture, the leading attraction will probably be toward this continental federation after it has fully taken shape.

Europe has no capital city and no government—yet. But her volunteers have fought side by side on Europe's battlefields and in the Underground, while in Germany there were millions of workers and prisoners sharing the same fate and preparing for the same liberation.

Such communion, never experienced before, would be enough to initiate a new era. Add to these emotions shared in a common experience the need of solidarity for self-preservation in the future. To make Europeans agree theoretically that solidarity was desirable has never been difficult.

Now solidarity has been achieved through vital common experience.

Today there are, in effect, five great powers who having fought the war against their common enemies are committed to the task of preserving the world's many civilizations.

They are the British Empire, China, Liberated Europe, Russia and the United States.

THE OTHER COMPONENTS

ENGLAND, RUSSIA

THE TEN UNITED NATIONS INSIDE EUROPE ARE THE FOUNDA-TION. To the east and to the west their two great allies, Russia and England, are the friendly powers who have everything to gain by the creation of a free and prosperous Europe.

In any European Council entrusted with the maintenance of peace on that continent and the organization of its normal exchanges, England and Russia, though not strictly European, will of course participate, thereby raising to 313 million the total number of Europeans who are immediately committed to the stabilization of European life.

Such a tripartite alliance is not a mere diplomatic combine. There are three solid reasons why it should be valid and authentic.

1. Western Europe has no cause for deep-seated conflict with England, and was saved by her lone stand in 1940. The democratic countries of Europe owe a debt to England, just as England is indebted to them for their popular resistance to the Nazis. Allied with England, they have nothing to fear from the east, nor has England anything to fear as long as she has ten faithful allies on the Continent. The days of her "splendid isolation" are forever past. Her ties with her dominions are ethnical, economic

and historical. But her very existence is bound to that of a free and strong Western Europe, and at last she knows it, because she almost lost that existence. From now on she is in Europe and of Europe.

2. The freed nations of Western and Central Europe are eager to resume normal relations with Russia, who through mutual distrust has been isolated for many years. The people feel that both the fear of a Russian scheme for world subversion and Western schemes for the annihilation of communism have lost their foundations. These plots belong to the past. Only an inordinate amount of blundering could revive them.

3. The Anglo-Russian alliance of 1942 is the keystone of European peace. According to its terms, it is to run for 20 years following the end of the war. As long as it lasts and is properly implemented, that any nation would yield to the temptation to break the peace is inconceivable. An Anglo-Russian alliance destroyed Napoleon; another broke Hitler's back. If anything can discourage future imitators, it is this concrete agreement, which nothing should be able to disrupt.

The Anglo-Russian frictions in the past had their cause in a rivalry of imperialistic ambitions, in which India, Afghanistan and Persia were the stakes. For nearly half a century, both Russia and England preferred to divide spheres of influence by orderly negotiation rather than to prepare for the "inevitable conflict." That conflict is by way of joining in oblivion the old inevitable conflict between the United States and Canada, when the slogan was "54° 40' or fight." There was no fight, and the frontier does not run along the 54° 40' parallel.

It is also worth noting that the Anglo-Russian alliance

was concluded by Mr. Churchill, whose party is certainly not too favorable to Russia. Should the fluctuations of internal politics bring other parties to the helm in England, the alliance has nothing to fear because these parties will be even more inclined to a policy of friendship with the Soviet Union.

A tripartite alliance between England, Russia and the ten liberated countries would fulfill almost exactly the function which in 1919 devolved upon the tripartite alliance between England, America and France. Wilson, whom it is the fashion to-day to accuse of a lack of realism, and Clemenceau, long blamed for his lack of idealism, agreed on the keystone of the peace of 1919: a definite commitment to put force in motion immediately in case of a German threat against peace. When America withdrew from world cooperation, the tripartite alliance went by the board, with many other things. Some "ifs" are open to doubt, but this one is not: if the tripartite agreement had been in force, there would have been no second world war.

This time, the peace of Europe should not and will not depend on the political mood of the American public. One experience is enough and the Europeans know it. They know that the American people wish peace, will never, in all probability, attempt anything against peace, and that American wealth, industry and manpower are the great reserves from which free nations can expect concrete assistance and moral support. But it is still too soon to expect American opinion to be ready to accept the quick moves that may be required in the Europe of the next decades. Moreover, American support is far more likely to be forthcoming if Europe knows what she wants and demonstrates responsibility. Therefore, whatever American commitments materialize after this war they will be and should be more in the nature of *reinsurance* of the European peace system than of a major responsibility in direct leadership.

The alliance of these twelve countries, of their 313 million people who are ready for it, is well-balanced. It would be hopeless for either Russia or England to attempt to dominate it exclusively. To carve spheres of influence that would bring East and West into opposition would be suicidal for both, and an invitation for Germany and her former satellites to revive a powerful Mitteleuropa, holding the balance between East and West. But there is another reason why such spheres cannot materialize. It is that the liberated countries are in no mood to "belong" to anyone's sphere.[1] As a matter of fact, the countries most likely to be pro-Russian are not Russia's immediate neighbors. Poland, Hungary and Rumania are less well disposed to Russian influence and leadership than Czechoslovakia and Yugoslavia, who are farther west.

But this is not the whole story.

Three other nations, who lost their political independence before hostilities started, may be expected to regain

[1] "We Czechs are democrats; our democratic institutions correspond to those of the British, the Americans, and the French of the Third Republic. We have never disguised the fact that Soviet ideology is different from ours, but we have never been afraid of the difference. . . . We are not exclusively pro-Russian. We look to the West again—so eagerly that we would regard the exclusion of France from the affairs of Europe as a blunder no less fatal than was the twenty years' exclusion of Soviet Russia. The Anglo-Soviet pact gives us the right assurance. The Czechs are pro-Anglo-Russian. I need hardly add that they are also pro-United States." (Jan Masaryk, Foreign Minister of Czechoslovakia, in *The Nation*, December 2, 1944).

it at the end of this war. They are Spain, Austria and Albania with their 34 millions of inhabitants. All three experienced German and Italian interference with their national freedom. All three are entitled to join a European confederation as soon as it takes shape, and their obvious interests demand that they should.

THE NEUTRALS, THE FORMER AXIS SATELLITES

Portugal, Sweden, Turkey (in Europe), Switzerland and Ireland have 21 million inhabitants. There is every reason why they should be invited to become associated with a European federation, on the same basis as the twelve neutral nations who were invited to join the League of Nations in 1919, and who accepted.

The original members of a European federation could be, therefore, 20 nations totaling 368 million people.

What remains is Italy, the other four Axis satellites (Rumania, Hungary, Bulgaria and Finland) and last, Germany.

These five ex-satellite nations comprise 81 million people. As Europeans they are, temporarily, second-rate factors; the quality of their conversion and assimilation will be the test of Europe's vitality.

It is impossible to guess what course Italy will adopt, partly because of the special and tragic circumstances in which she finds herself, partly because of the extreme mobility of the Italian character. Whatever stand Italy takes, nothing can assure us that this stand will not be reversed after a brief period of time. Is it not to be expected, however, that due to the very nature of their genius, the Italians will be good Europeans if Europe itself is strong? For once, their foreign policy would be in harmony with their true national aspirations which are certainly peaceful. It took plenty of bad statesmanship—too clever, therefore bad —to make Italy the ally of a militaristic Germany twice in two generations. Suppress military Germany, and Italian statesmanship will be freed from like temptations, and will return to the "real Italian" tradition of Mazzini.[1] But whatever position Italy will occupy in the future, it is too soon for the ten liberated nations to regard her as one of them.

Neither Italy nor the other Axis ex-satellites should be considered as more than passive members of a European federation at the start. For civic consciousness or international maturity, these nations cannot be compared to the fighting Allies. But if Fascism and Nazism are destroyed and out of the picture, a vast majority of these unfortunate people, recently chained to the German war-chariot, will turn in hope toward our Europe. I am thinking of their peasants who have been exploited by cliques of politicians and unworthy "ruling classes." Unlike the Prussians, they have no vocation for killing, plundering and enslaving. They are passive and have shown that they could follow the wrong leaders, but their children may prove to be as good Europeans as any others, once their countries resume their natural course of evolution.

[1] "The Italian apostles of the idea of nationality never considered nations to be ends in themselves. In his struggle, Mazzini never ceased to affirm that the triumph of nationalities should finally be crowned by a European union." (C. Sforza, *The Real Italians*.)

AND NOW GERMANY

Is it true, as some people believe, that "everything" will depend upon what the 26th country will say or do, or will not do? Is a strong and healthy Europe "inconceivable" without Germany as its main prop and central feature?

Is not the answer to the German problem entirely implied in the answer to the European problem? In the midst of an orderly Europe of 521 million people, Germany is no longer a mighty, fearful power, bigger than any of her neighbors. She is a minority of 66 million people—that is, less than 13% of the whole. If the ten liberated nations want a Europe, if their great fighting Allies want it too, if the neutrals want it and if the unwilling vassals of the Axis secretly wish it to materialize, then does it matter so much whether this Europe is welcome or unwelcome to the Germans? What matters is that the fine plans for the next war of the Generals von Stuelpnagel, von Rundstedt and von Mannstein, the schemes expressed in the *Voelkische Beobachter* and the *Schwarze Korps*,[1] automatically become zero.

As a matter of fact, the memory of these plans will keep Europeans together should they ever be tempted to forget or forgive, or to relax from their necessary vigilance before a new generation of real Europeans has been brought up, and aggressive Germany has been buried. It should be enough to recall how nearly the German plans succeeded, and to remember the primary condition for their success: a Europe divided between East and West.

Against this division, human cement is provided by the ten liberated nations. To England and Russia, division

[1] See page 45.

means great risks. To the ten nations it means certain death.[1]

[1] From Winston Churchill's address to the House of Commons on March 21, 1943:

". . . In Europe dwell the historic parent races from whom our Western civilization has been so largely derived.

". . . We must try to make the Council of Europe, or whatever it may be called, into a really effective league with all the strongest forces concerned woven into its texture, with a high court to adjust disputes and with forces, armed forces, national or international or both, held ready to enforce these decisions and prevent renewed aggressions and the preparation of future wars.

". . . It is my earnest hope that we shall achieve the largest common measure of the integrated life of Europe that is possible without destroying the individual characteristics and traditions of its many ancient and historic races. All this will, I believe, be found to harmonize with the high permanent interests of Britain, the United States and Russia."

STRUCTURE AND POLICIES

It is generally assumed that Europe is and has always been a maze of insoluble problems. Granted the problems and granted the maze, I take exception to the word insoluble. Mankind has spent its long life working out one problem after another. New ones have always sprung up. But whenever there was a will to dispose of them, there was a way.

Who would have said that Greeks and Turks could ever become good neighbors? That Soviet Russia would become an ally of the Western democracies? Who, forty years ago, would have expected the Boers to fight at the side of the British, or the Filipinos with the Yankees? Or the French industrial worker, the village priest, the school teacher and the officer-aristocrat to become comrades in arms in the same guerrilla band?

Hitler has united many people who thought they were enemies. We have seen the merging, or at least the alliance of many traditions which were regarded as exclusive of each other: the religious and the socialist, the patriot and the humanitarian.

Now, a number of Europeans have begun to love Europe. This is the second great historico-psychological fact in this century. The first, twenty-five years ago, was that a majority of men became consciously disgusted with war and indifferent to conquest. Here is where new eyes are required, to perceive the new position of our old problems.

THE FRONTIERS

Let there be no illusion about seeing frontiers abolished in our lifetime. Whether it would be a generous idea or not, the people concerned are not in the required mood. But frontiers are not necessarily fighting fronts or economic barriers. They may become simple administrative divisions like the frontier between Kentucky and Indiana. Many frontiers in Europe were "entpolitisiert," even when the boundary line looked queer on the map. All that is needed is that no irredentism should remain and that economic exchange across the line should conform to the lasting interests of people on both sides, as it does, for instance, on the Canada-United States boundary line. Contrary to the general American belief, there were thousands of miles of satisfactory frontiers in Europe. Look at the map of Geneva. Surrounded by hills which are on French territory, it is separated from its hinterland, yet there is no irredentism, no claim or threat from either side. The frontier cuts across populations who speak the same language, and Geneva is dependent on a foreign country, France, for its commercial outlets and even for its food. Nevertheless, peace and good will have prevailed in that region for centuries and nobody wishes to change the status quo. The same applied to the Franco-Belgian, Franco-Spanish, Swiss-German, Swedish-Norwegian, and many other frontiers.

It may be surprising to hear that European frontiers, in the future, should not be very different from those of 1919. Yes, the "Wilsonian" frontiers. Apart from the Sudeten irredentism which was entirely and artificially fabricated in a few weeks by Hitler in 1938, there were probably not two million people out of three hundred million, west of Warsaw, who complained of imposed national allegiance. There were at least twenty European countries who did not dream of acquiring anybody else's territory. This fact did not make the headlines. It was the few troublesome nations who created the impression prevalent in America, of a hopeless pandemonium of claims and counterclaims.

There are few more dangerous booby-traps than the cliché that 1919 frontiers were "senseless," "vengeful," a source for future conflicts, and so on. German propaganda peddled that cliché with remarkable tenacity in America, and was rewarded with a considerable degree of success. Yet by the provisions of 1919, some fifty-five million Europeans were freed from foreign rule.[1] That is not an achievement to be ashamed of, and to repudiate without qualification. It is untrue that boundaries then set up were unworkable, or that the national units created in 1918 by the will of their people rather than by the initiative of diplomats could not live. Look at the growth of Belgrade, of Bucharest and of Prague, whose population fairly doubled in the two decades following the dissolution of Austria-Hungary.

The economic structure of Europe did not keep pace with its political organization. But in many instances, either the much-calumniated men of Versailles or the services of the League produced solutions to the so-called insoluble problems. And they worked: plebiscite areas, Saar administration, Silesian partition, Aland islands, minority petitions, etc. More often than not, these were international solutions.

[1] Poles, Czechoslovaks, Rumanians, Serbs, Croats, Slovenes, Italians, Alsatians and Danes.

When I discussed with my students of International Politics some complicated situation involving mixed races and languages, conflicting traditions and interests, someone generally rose to suggest "an international solution"; some sort of joint authority, temporary or permanent, with a police force to discourage the troublemakers. The students were aware of similar orderly procedures which had succeeded in many cases. These were procedures which did not make front-page news; the front-page news was for the failures and the acts of violence.

People say glibly that our peace system was "unworkable." Yet as a matter of fact, out of sixty nations who signed the pact renouncing war as an instrument of national policy in 1928, only three violated it before 1939: Japan, Italy and Germany. None of them will be in a position to do so again, for some time. Is it too optimistic to expect that the other nations, who kept their word before and solved *all* their many differences peacefully, may persevere in that course after the law-breakers are crushed and disarmed?

New troubles will loom up, difficult and terrible perhaps, with no ready answers. There may be social clashes of a new kind, new ways of oppressing the individual man, worse forms of intellectual barbarity, perhaps, or of collective fanaticism. I am not blind to the frightful prospects for our civilization if it should abandon itself to some of its present trends. But I insist that international conflicts leading to war can be stopped and solved, not only because it is in the interest of an overwhelming majority—it always was—but because to-day that majority is aware of its power to prevent war—at least in Europe.

In other words, I believe in a higher maturity of European international thinking. This may seem absurd to those accustomed to the idea of a backward, benighted Europe, torn with inexplicable fears and feuds. Yet I have confidence in young Europeans who have been saturated with hard and cruel experience and who want desperately to live and love and work at peace.

AIMS OF NATIONAL POLICIES

Assuming that each European nation retains most of its responsibility in the conduct of its foreign policy, what will those policies be like?

There are three kinds of foreign policies.

The most primitive is based on the notion that all strangers are enemies. As a consequence, if a neighbor appears weak, you attack him. If he is stronger than you, you submit to him, because there is no alternative except suicide—and some tribes preferred suicide.

Foreign relations of another sort are those in which each nation considers the others as merely potential enemies. In the intervals between wars, they carry on negotiations to build up alliances against the most dangerous of their neighbors. They work on the assumption that they can expect the worst from anyone at any time, but that a "balance of power" can endure for a period, during which children are born and men die of natural causes. Every year of peace is a miraculous and undeserved gift of fate. Out of such a policy has grown a kind of statesmanship which requires some imagination, but it is not statesmanship of the highest order.

The third type of foreign policy is founded on the proposition that wars are not acts of God but are man-made, and can be prevented by other men. It is a realistic policy, in that it looks around for as many people and nations as can be gathered together, who will share in the serious enterprise of keeping and enforcing the peace. It takes up the problem of the "Cause and cure of war" and says:

1. The cause of war is that it pays—sometimes.
2. The cure is to see that it does not pay—at any time.

This sounds simple, but there are people who will tell you it is not realistic.

I believe that most Europeans had come to this point of view twenty years ago. They were waiting for the greater, more prosperous nations to realize these simple facts of life. Hitler struck before these great nations had seen the point. He could strike, in fact, *because* they had not yet seen it.

The outside world, we hear, is planning to send educators to Europe. Here are a few things they do *not* need to teach most Europeans:

1. That if war breaks out in one place, there is no telling how far it will spread,
2. That disunion and piecemeal action bring disaster,
3. That with one tenth of the indomitable courage and one hundredth of the sacrifices consented to by nations once they are threatened with destruction, these same nations can establish and preserve a peaceful world, at little cost and no risk. The outside world discovered these facts by 1944. To the liberated nations they are not exactly new.

Yet in America, these truths have produced a confusing abundance of ill-defined proposals, probably because many people and most politicians have tried to tackle and to dodge them at the same time.

FORCE

The principle formulated in article X of the League Covenant [1] was half-implemented in article XVI, which commits nations to economic sanctions but leaves military sanctions to the discretion of each sovereign state. As early as 1919 the plain people of Europe understood that a society of nations should be fully empowered and pledged to use force against the use of force. But the English public did not realize this fully before 1934 (the "Peace Ballot" campaign, following the rise of Hitler). The American public, in its majority, has not realized it fully yet. This was amply proved at recent primaries, party conventions, and local elections of 1944.

The right and obligation to use force against aggressors is what make the difference between a going concern and a mere debating or juridical body unable to make its decisions respected.

Europeans, as their first choice, would like to see a world league, with universal membership and collective participation to international duties. But if such a league does not materialize immediately, or takes the shape of a loose partnership with reduced responsibilities, or of a mere alliance between a few large powers, then Europeans, as their second choice, will form their own league. They have been ready a long time. They expected the

---

[1] Text of article X: "The members of the League undertake to respect and preserve as against external aggression the territorial integrity and existing political independence of all members of the League. In case of any such aggression or in case of any threat or danger of such aggression the council shall advise upon the means by which this obligation shall be fulfilled."

necessary commitments to be taken in 1919. This time they will not wait. It is safe to predict that a close system of military security and mutual protection will exist between the ten liberated nations, and between them and England and Russia.

The main lines of such a system are no mystery and no novelty. We worked on them as early as 1931, before the Conference on the Reduction of Armaments. Hitler's unchecked rise to power, and German rearmament relegated all such plans, including the Conference itself, to a utopian dream.[1]

To clarify the whole problem, let it be stated first that the enforcement of peace implies two kinds of international force. One corresponds to the police in our communities. It should be small, mobile and highly efficient—professionals doing a full-time job. Its duty is to be ready at all times to maintain order, quell limited disturbances, intervene when local forces lack prestige or unity of purpose, throw a neutral zone between neighbors whose feelings are running high, etc.

The other force is what would be required to check a deliberate aggression by a whole nation. Such a force must be large enough to defeat the armies of a big country. A force of that size could not be kept permanently mobilized without excessive expenditure and even some

[1] See text of the telegram addressed to the German delegation by Arthur Henderson, British Labor leader and president of the Conference.
Apart from the documents of the Conference itself, the most constructive proposals concerning an international force were presented by a committee headed by Senator H. de Jouvenel and formulated by Pierre Denis in the magazine *Politique,* November, 1931. I summed up these proposals in an article for the Washington *Post*, March 24, 1935.

ridicule attached to it if the need for it never arose. It must consist of the potential forces of all nations concerned, and if the emergency is great, as in 1914 and 1939, the joint contributions may amount to the total armed forces of the law-abiding nations, entering into action immediately, not three years after the aggression.

There is no getting away from this latter possibility. Citizens of the world must know that they are all liable to service against a new Hitler. It is that very liability, clearly recognized and accepted, which will make a new Hitler impossible.

Foch's international army, and Eisenhower's international army, are precisely such forces. They would not have had to materialize if law-breaker William II and law-breaker Hitler had known in advance, with certainty, that these armies existed.

Many people today will admit of a small international police force, but try to evade the universal obligation to take up arms against a large-scale aggression. It is like saying that we shall have policemen to run after petty thieves, but we cannot afford to cope with gangsters.

If the world is not ready for the necessary commitments, the ten liberated nations will limit theirs to Europe. But they cannot and will not dispense with them.

Now the practical implementing of such a general principle may be simpler than a total conscription of every man, woman and child for service in the armed forces. But to evade the principle because it is new (or rather, was new in 1919) will lead us nowhere. And the ghost of article X will come back and haunt our statesmen, as long as our public does not recognize it as an unescapable necessity of the modern world.

THE PRACTICAL ENFORCEMENT OF ORDER

To answer the need for an international enforcement of law and order, there is need for *two* types of forces, as entirely distinct from each other as a peacetime constabulary and a mobilized national army. These two are almost always confused when the subject of an international force is brought up.

1. Police force. A European permanent international police force of some 50,000 men should be sufficient after peace is restored. When each country is again fully able to care for its own internal peace and order, it could be reduced to a small general reserve.

In the meantime, this force could be garrisoned in a dozen places in the vicinity of important centers of communication from which detachments could be moved to wherever their presence was required, either for a "token" appearance, or as a concentrated move of several units in case of regional emergency. Each unit would have approximately the strength of the international force which held the Saar region during the plebiscite of 1935. Among places suitable for the permanent stationing of these units, one might suggest Antwerp, Danzig, Lwow, Salonica, Trieste, etc.

Members of the police force would be recruited from *all* European countries (all should be represented), but not on a proportional basis in relation to population. On the contrary, it is desirable that the largest number should come from small countries with a high standard of civic education. Men should not be garrisoned in their land of origin.

Carefully selected and serving for a long term, highly

trained and well paid, this European police force should be able to deal efficiently with any local international disturbance or state of tension. Again, it can *not* deal with a whole aggressor nation choosing war as the instrument of its policy.

2. *International force against aggression.* As we said before, the underlying principle must be that a total mobilization of all European nations *could* be required, if necessary—against a new Hitler, for instance. The scheme, worked out in 1931, reduces the problem to lesser proportions.

Today, just as the greatest menace from an aggressor would probably come from his use of air force, the capacity for prevention also lies with air force.

This weapon, dangerous in the hands of an aggressor, would be equally efficient in the hands of the peace-enforcing community. It is the same improved tommy-gun that makes the gangster dangerous and the police efficient.

In the present scheme, there is more than merely entrusting the European confederation with an air force. There are three distinct steps to be taken:

1. As a prerequisite for general security, there must be a general limitation of national air forces and more particularly of the number of bombers to be retained by each nation. European nations do not wish to embark on a new race of armaments and will have to agree on respective "ceilings," as did the naval powers at the Washington Conference of 1921–22. This is imperative for reasons of economy as well as of elementary security.

2. An agreement to place all commercial aviation under European joint control or supervision.

3. As a complement to these measures, the creation of a European air force, sufficiently powerful to break any attempt at aggression, even by one of the big nations. The mastery of the air over Europe must not be an object of competition; it must belong to Europe, in the interest of all.

Individual nations may keep strong fighter forces for their protection, but the long-range bombing force should be under direct federal authority, although stationed in the various countries and ready to participate in their protection.

The placing of commercial aviation under European control is intended first as a measure of economic efficiency,[1] and second in order to keep individual nations from the temptation of building commercial planes with a view to their transformation into war planes, airfields with offensive military purposes, etc. The patchwork of European frontiers is incompatible with the growth of independent national aviation. National regulations and general competition would either paralyze the normal development of air lines, or ruin the taxpayers. For prestige and for military purposes, each nation used to subsidize air lines duplicating those of other nations, at the same time creating a military danger for those nations.

The management of European commercial aviation would be under an international board, like the "Compagnie Internationale des Wagons Lits." Above the whole organization there would be a "European Air Union" comparable to the Postal Union existing at present. The sev-

[1] Europe must avoid a condition of economic anarchy, waste, and high costs to the public, such as may result from so-called "free competition" when it actually results in huge combines keeping public services at a low degree of efficiency.

eral governments would delegate their authority to that Union in matters of commercial aviation.

It is easy to see what the result would be for security if on one hand military aviation were largely under direct federal control, on the other hand commercial aviation were operated without any ulterior preoccupation of military use.

The European air force would be complemented by the land forces which all European nations must be pledged to contribute in case of grave trouble. But it may well be that the very existence of a strong air force would be sufficient to make aggression hopeless. No matter what degree of efficiency the German Army had attained on September 1, 1939, would Hitler have given the order to invade Poland if he had known for certain that within 24 hours the whole military aviation of Europe would be strafing his advancing columns? Hours, not days or months or years.

For a nation threatened with attack, what makes air assistance particularly valuable is

1. That it is extremely quick in arriving
2. That it involves a comparatively small number of men, all trained for the job, and does not raise the two great objections to the use of sanctions: the disruption of normal life on a vast scale, and the lack of readiness of public opinion.

The slow, expensive, awkward mobilization of huge land forces in many countries for the defense of one of them, is what the aggressor hopes will deter peace-loving nations from interfering with his plans. So the aggressor may win a complete victory before sanctions become effective. But airplanes, ready for action in fifteen countries or more, speeding to the support of the nation attacked, and getting there before the invader has secured any serious advantage, that is another matter. It is not only feasible, it is easy to imagine—even for the aggressor.

In the future, it may be the prospect and fear of such immediate action that will discourage aggression.

LEAGUES OLD AND NEW

Anybody who is *not* a utopian knows that there will be some sort of world organization after this war.

There are great arguments as to "what kind of a League" we shall have.

The answer is: more than one kind.

There is more than one kind of need to be satisfied, since nations, as regards world unity, have not reached the same degree of evolution.

It is imperative that there be:

1. A relatively loose alliance between all powers willing to act together in case of grave emergency. That is a maximum of solidarity with a minimum of renunciation of sovereignty and free action. Such an alliance is indispensable if the world is to escape either anarchy through unregulated rivalries, or new attempts at domination. It would be the kind of League which corresponds to present-day advanced American thinking, or British thinking around 1924—that is, general principles and limited commitments. The conference at Dumbarton Oaks proved that both Russia and the U.S., although willing to shoulder important responsibilities, are reluctant to subordinate their acts to a vote by other nations, and insisted on retaining their sovereign right of veto. As a result, we shall have some-

thing similar to the concert of great powers established in Europe in 1815, or to the "concert européen" of the late 19th century. It will mean a little less than the League of Nations of 1919, in principle, but may amount to a little more in efficacy because it will include the U.S. and Russia from the start.

2. A more tightly knit League of the nations who have fought on the same side in this war and are strongly determined, by collective effort and explicit readiness to act, to prevent a renewal of war. This means England, Russia and as many others as will be ready to join in a pledge for mutual protection.

3. Still closer ties bind the ten continental nations which we called "the hard core of Europe." They are already, implicitly, one single great power in the process of being liberated. They accept their solidarity, not as a newly discovered necessity as Americans accept their world commitments, but as a long dreamed-of goal, foreseen for centuries by the best among their thinkers and leaders.

Liberated Europe will preserve, of course, its alliances with England and Russia, and its looser ties with the U.S. and China. But it must count primarily on itself for immediate protection, and will organize accordingly.[1]

There is, of course, no conflict between these various and interlocking associations of nations, any more than there is a conflict between having a good town police and *also* a solid bolt on your door. If this is made quite clear, the outlook for the world League is quite hopeful. Common sense demands it. Common sense demanded it 25

[1] This is a return to the notion formulated over ten years ago by Paul Boncour: that of "concentric circles" of decreasing commitments, tight for nations of the inner circle, looser for the remote and less concerned ones.

years ago, but as long as big nations did not recognize it, it was merely truth in the abstract. In our world, truth in the abstract cannot die, but it may be kept waiting in the cold outside the gates for a very long time indeed. Since December 7, 1941, this truth has been brought home to almost everybody.

There used to be a world reality and an American reality, and when the two did not fit, Americans were inclined to dismiss the outside reality as, shall we say, non-Euclidean. Since December '41 the two realities have merged into one. America and the world, if they do not yet speak the same language, at least have agreed on how to spell the word "danger."

As can be seen, both the tight European system and the loose world system which are now in the making, have this feature in common: no single power can boss either of them. All this does not automatically take the place of responsible citizenship and responsible thinking. But it makes quite a difference if we start with a sensible structure, really world-wide this time.

To Europeans, this is not exactly a *new* hope. It is the hope of 1919, presented under better auspices. But as the memory of the desperate disappointment of 1920 is still present with us, it may be expected that Europe will prefer two precautions to one, and that she will endorse both the world security schemes, with participation of all, and the European, home-made and much tighter security provisions.

EUROPEAN ECONOMY

The cautious suggestions presented by Briand in 1929, towards the creation of a "federal tie" between European nations, were largely based on economic motives as well as preoccupations of security.

Briand had been accused of idealism, day-dreaming, etc. Therefore, he wished to keep away from vague propositions, and to establish the foundations of a new Europe on material advantages for all the participants, such as a freer flow of goods, unhampered access to raw materials, a closer cooperation between industrial and agricultural regions. In other words, everything the Americans had done inside their continent after they had suppressed barriers and restrictions to interstate trade. A committee for the study of European union was created. But after Wall Street had sent us a first-class financial and economic depression, nations like individuals fell back on the emergency measures intended to give them immediate protection against collapse. Things went rapidly from bad to worse, and Europe emerged from the economic crisis to find herself confronted with the rise of Hitler, himself a product of that crisis. Briand had died, and European union had become a forgotten hope.

A paradox of this situation is that everyone who gave a thought to the matter expected Germany to benefit more than any other country by the plan. Sitting in the center of Europe, amply equipped industrially and with good markets all around, she would have profited greatly by a stimulation of inter-European trade. Stresemann saw it. Hitler was not interested, having other plans, and plotted wonderful shortcuts towards the happiness of the German people whom he loved so well.

The moral of this story is that Europe can and will probably be reconstructed without Germany. Although Germany will ultimately find her place in it, her share will never be what was within her easy reach in 1929. Some opportunities do not ring twice.

Economic planning for Europe does not require such vast imaginative powers as world economic planning. Raising 800 million Chinese and Hindus to a higher standard of living and buying capacity, with the expected and the unexpected consequences, is a task that will cover decades. Organizing Europe means the abolition of artificial fetters, which were of profit to very few. There was a time, which I remember, when Europe enjoyed practically international currency, because the silver units of a dozen countries were accepted everywhere; not to mention the gold which was of current use and a true international money. Passports were not required except to enter Russia and Turkey. We have gone a long way backwards since 1913.

To conceive European economy as a whole is not beyond the powers of the average citizen or statesman of our countries. No revolutionary upsetting of our traditions is necessary. Before this war, a gradual lowering of tariffs would have been needed in order to avoid sudden shocks to legitimate interests. Since everything has been shocked and disturbed, we shall begin with no trade at all. It should be easier to start on the right foot. Again, the best example to follow is that of the United States after their emancipation. Nobody will deny that the process was successful. We should remember that this process was not adopted without spirited resistance on the part of the States, or rather certain private interests in most of the States. What the U.S. Congress could agree upon, one hundred and sixty years ago, should not prove insuperable for a European Congress, especially as little "big interests" will be very much under fire (this is hardly a metaphor) in the days following Europe's liberation.

As to the integration of European economy into a larger world economy, that is beyond the scope of the present book. But inter-European economy should not raise very controversial issues. Some initial moves will be dictated by emergency plus common sense. Inter-European trade relations are based on long traditions; governments and privileged interests often did more to paralyze than to promote them. If a general basis for broad principles is needed, it can be found in the recommendations of the economic world conference of the League in 1927. Their conclusions can apply immediately to Europe.

Given the mood of the ten liberated nations, it is not likely that any of them will be open to economic "colonization" from the outside, even should it be attempted by friendly interests. These nations will be jealous of their independence in all its forms and their people will exert a far more searching and exacting supervision than heretofore, of the deals and contracts that might even remotely place their national resources under foreign control. They will perhaps carry this to excess, but it must be realized as a fact. Certain interests and perhaps even some governments, will be willing to consider deals. Such a course will place them very soon at a disadvantage with national opinion, while national legislation will undoubtedly become extremely strict on such matters. This will constitute a stumbling block—not to international trade on a basis of equal opportunities, but to any "special influence" granted to any non-European interests. In other words, Europe will be no ground for *privileged* economic penetration by anyone, and the best way to reap large profits from trading with any given European country will be to cooperate in promoting active trade all around. It is a simple and sound principle, recognized long ago within the limits of domestic business. It will have to prevail also beyond our frontiers.

"POPULAR FRONTS"

It requires no great foresight to tell that if there is going to be leadership "of the people by the people and for the people" anywhere, it will be in the ten liberated countries of Europe. Everything points to a prospect of democracy radical and uncompromising—for better or for worse.

Regimes may be ruthless or tolerant, they may be efficient or not. One sure thing is that the people will keep a close watch on their operation. The future will be a great test of democracy. There will no longer be a democracy of general principles working through routine institutions amidst general apathy, but a total democracy jealously controlled by people who had lost it, are regaining it, and therefore know exactly what it is worth to them.

There used to be two classes of people in the world: those who never had real democracy, and those who never had it taken away from them. Neither class could truly appraise it. To-day, Europe can.

The term "popular front" is probably what describes best the ruling regimes of to-morrow in Europe. I know that it evokes all sorts of monstrous and distorted images for some people: mobs on the rampage, uncontrolled strikes, industry paralyzed, wealth confiscated—and that to others it spells the promised land, all evils abolished and easy money for everybody. In reality, popular front

simply means coalition of the Leftist parties, therefore "total democracy." It seems bound to happen because:
1. The Leftist parties control a majority of the votes in practically all of the countries concerned.
2. Some of the Rightist parties have been discredited by collaboration with the temporary conquerors.[1]
3. There are few if any cases where a single leftist party control a majority. Therefore the leftists must form a coalition among themselves, or relinquish leadership.

Regardless of socialist inefficiency, real or supposed, in achieving political success, the underlying prestige of true socialism must be great indeed, since anti-socialist parties like the Nazis and the Communists chose to borrow the name. Lenin's regime called Russia a union of "socialist soviet republics" although no socialists were allowed there. Hitler called "nazional-sozialist" a regime whose main purpose was to destroy socialism. This homage to socialist prestige seems, however, an insult to the intelligence of the socialist voters . . .[2]

The fact remains that there are socialist and socialist-labor parties everywhere in the Liberated Nations and most neutral countries,[3] and that as a rule they correspond

[1] This does not mean that a host of patriots and some excellent leaders did not arise from the "Right." But *as parties* their complacency to fascism and their unfailing instinct in betting on the wrong horse on every occasion have ruined their present qualification for leadership. An intelligent conservatism, however, is not unthinkable in some future. Its rise will depend on two factors: the sober training of conservatives in the understanding of the world which is around them, and on the other hand the extent of the mistakes which the popular front regimes will undoubtedly make.

[2] Similar instances, less successful: French rightists calling themselves "Républicains de gauche," American isolationists calling themselves "progressives."

[3] 50% of Parliament in Sweden, for instance.

to the "middle-of-the-road" in the popular front, that is, between democrats and communists. In most countries, therefore, the political *center of gravity of the majority* falls within the socialist party, as it did, for instance, in France after the last elections (1936). It would not be surprising, therefore, if the socialists held the balance of power in Liberated Europe as a whole. It would be far better if our friends abroad did not consider this as either a millennium or a cataclysm. It is simply the outcome of a very gradual process, as slowly achieved as the rise of the Labor party in England over the last 60 years.

CONVERGENCE OF VALID TRADITIONS

The most important change in European political life may not be so much a new alignment of parties as a new attitude of the parties toward each other. There have been other landslides or semi-landslides to the left, throughout two centuries, with people wondering each time if the world was coming to an end. But never, on such a scale, have men of such varied and conflicting ideologies had the experience of being violently thrown together and fighting side by side.

It is not only people from ten nations who have come to know one another, as comrades-in-arms of the great rebellion. It is people belonging to different traditions, within each country, who have come to regard each other with respect.

Great European traditions are many; they co-existed in spite of their mutual opposition, and will continue to do so. But for the first time in history, instead of working at cross-purposes, they have worked together.

What are these traditions? We have the old aristocratic and military tradition which demands that one does not surrender as long as fighting is still possible. The Christian tradition, Catholic and Protestant alike, demands that men resist any attempt to enslave their souls, and maintains the supremacy of spiritual allegiance over worldly allegiance. Then, the great democratic and rationalistic tradition of the eighteenth century, demanding that people fight for the Rights of Man, which the French proclaimed in 1789 and which have become articles of faith for hundreds of millions the world over. Last, the socialist and humanitarian tradition, over a hundred years old, demands peace and social justice. All are obviously incompatible with Hitler's "New Order"; so that men formed by either one of these four great traditions are drawn toward the cause of a free Europe.

It will be strange if after they have offered their lives for Europe's salvation, they become so absent-minded that they let her drift into disunion, sell herself piecemeal to the highest bidder, submit to conquest in any form, and waste our new and splendid chances of security and prosperity.

THE SPIRITUAL FUNCTION OF EUROPE

From these abbreviated remarks, and tentative conclusions, it may be seen that my position, regarding the future of Europe, is one of conditional optimism. I have tried to outline the features of a newly living Europe, no longer a collective abstraction but as real as Scotland, or Athens. It is, of course, beyond my power to tell whether the young thing will flourish, become diseased and die, or be assassinated before it grows up. All I can say is that it is born healthy and should live.

Europe's place among the human communities of this world is not difficult to envisage. It has been prepared for a long time. Europe has the largest population of all single groups. Her arts, sciences and industries have influenced the whole earth, and her political thinking, resulting in "democracy the inevitable," after two victorious wars which saw the defeat of both imperial and totalitarian ideologies, is prevailing all over the world.

"Little Europe," therefore (which is larger than the United States and has four and a half times its population), is more than ever a focus of power and a source of human inspiration. It is not sure that its importance is doomed to disappear in a more or less remote future, although it is true that it is no longer alone in wielding power and influence.

But whatever Europe's statistical rank will be in terms of production or wealth or armaments, her main function, the irreplaceable one, is and will continue to be of a quite different nature. Just as the Mediterranean world of old exerted an influence out of proportion to its size, the quality of thinking originating in Europe is without its equivalent in the rest of the world.

This Europe which is born of a war of independence has more than one point in common with revolutionary America of 170 years ago. Men of the young United States passed through a supreme ordeal, a test of courage and reason, of tenacity and daring, of the loftiest and of the most realistic conceptions. So also have the Europeans of to-day been tested. The choice they made was dictated by their deepest allegiance, the allegiance to the liberty of their souls. Americans who had made a similar choice produced some of the highest statesmanship the world has known, and exerted an influence comparable to no other. Yet they were very few. I believe that the men and women of Europe will emerge with qualities similar to those which characterized the "founding fathers," because of their similar experience in war and responsibility.

GERMANY

Said a German officer taken prisoner in Normandy: "When I saw the invasion fleet covering the sea, the thousands of planes in the skies, I felt: 'God, I must in some way belong to a force like that!'"

NATURE OF THE GERMANS

THE GERMAN PROBLEM IS FIRST OF ALL A PART OF THE European problem, and its solution is and should be a corollary of the European solution.

The Germans should be—no, not slaughtered, but drowned in a healthy and peaceful Europe, where they will be one seventh of the total population. They will become orderly Europeans *once there is no alternative*.

This calls for an explanation, which is fundamental since it has to do with the nature of the German people.

Who are the Germans?

For centuries, that undefined region called Germany was a battlefield, a market-place and a general meeting-ground for all the European races and a few Asiatic ones. Many wars brought many people from many lands to Germany. During the Thirty Years War, Frederick the Great's campaigns and Napoleon's occupation, Frenchmen, Swedes, Russians, Poles, Hungarians, Bohemians, Croats, Italians, Swiss, Spaniards and a few others lived there and left many descendants.

Of these ten races, four are Slavic and three Mediterranean. Hitler talking about racial purity proves only that the Germans can believe anything said by anybody provided he is their master. And history shows that the Germans will accept anybody as their master.

German people show traces of every influence and germs of every possibility, as their behavior proves. They nourish all the ferments. No other people have shown themselves capable of such varieties of good and evil. They have no limits, no definite contours. Such a condition can lead to greatness, or to damnation. It may produce Goethe, that triumph of creative serenity, or pan-germanism, that glorified kleptomania, that boundless gluttony.

Are not the Germans famous for their good humor and for their brutality? For their faithfulness and for their urge to cheat? For their music and for their vulgarity? For the idealism of their dreams and the bestiality of their vices? They crave order and they upset Europe every thirty-five years. They plunder and torture and they wish to be loved. Their courage is great and they obey abjectly anyone who kicks them hard.

Why?

Because the Germans do not exist, as responsible individuals.

Scientifically, economically, the Germans think in 20th century terms. Politically, in terms of the 17th. Their political aims and ethical beliefs still shift from one object to another according to orders from above, or as events suggest, but not according to some election from within. After 1919, they protested against the Polish Corridor as the greatest scandal of the Versailles Treaty. In 1933 Hitler needed peace with Poland, before he was ready to attack her. The docile Germans immediately ceased to feel indignant about the Corridor. They resumed their indignation when they were told to. In 1929, not a German out of a thousand dreamt of annexing the Sudetenland. At a sign from above, they would have been willing to regard the English or French as noble partners in world domination, as they did the Japanese, honorary Aryans. They are politically fluid. They take the form of whatever they are poured into. To become instead of to be. They have no specific national temperament, like a Turk, a Spaniard, a Norwegian, a Scot. A German's choice is always determined by external decisions or circumstances.

Hitler in power is a product of German political nonexistence and of the economic crisis. For once, historical materialism is right. Why do people talk about the "mystical" motives of his followers? They followed because he was winning. But it is true that to the Germans, victory and success have a mystical value in themselves. This is a pre-mediaeval attitude which antedates chivalry and modern notions of honor. It has not yet occurred to the Germans that a victory may be dishonorable or a defeat glorious. That is why Hitler had to create the myth of the undefeated German armies of 1918. We considered that the German armies had fought extremely well, and that no shame was attached to that defeat. The Germans on the other hand did not feel dishonorable when violating Belgian neutrality which they had guaranteed, because they were successful. They felt dishonored because they lost the war. In order to regain their honor they needed a lie: that the Jews and the Socialists had stabbed their armies in the back. They loved Hitler because he formulated the lie for them.

If deep authentic motives had produced Hitler, people would have rallied to him in 1923 when Germany was downtrodden, lonely and humiliated, and had genuine national motives for desperate action. In 1930, peace prevailed, no one threatened Germany, Europe was preparing to disarm, authority was relaxed and Europeans would be slow to wake up to danger. Then Hitler had his chance.

Germany's economic depression of 1930 was particularly severe because her bankers and industrialists had imitated the worst features of American speculation and unwarranted financial optimism, without the rich American margin of resources. People did not understand what was happening. So they turned to Hitler because he had an explanation. The critical powers of a child of ten should have sufficed to see that the explanation was one hundred percent untrue and unsubstantiated. But the Germans as citizens have no critical powers. They agreed that it was all because of democracy, the foreigners, free speech and the Jews.

Anti-Semitism is a crusade of people with inferiority complexes.

Anti-Semitism is a disease that grows on brains that are unwashed and on hearts which are not clean.

There is not a single example of a really great man who ever descended to anti-Semitism.

Anti-Semitism, Fascism, Nazism which go hand in hand, never succeed in prosperous or well-balanced communities. They thrive on fear and discouragement.

What explains Germany of to-day, and the irresistible appeal that violence has for the German soul, is the memory of the colossal profits derived from the use of force in the past. Germans cannot help remembering all that they reaped through violence in 1864, 1866, 1871, 1914, 1938 and 1940.

So that even when Germany lost a war as in 1918, what the Germans remembered was the long period of successful plunder, and what remains deep in them is the hope that it can be resumed. In the last war German victories and profiteering lasted four years, German defeat only a few weeks.

National memory is molded by such facts. From 1814 on, war has meant, to a German, fighting on someone else's soil. Each officer becomes a lord, and each general a sovereign. To French, Belgian or Polish people, war means invasion of their land, a tide of refugees, trenches dug in their fields. In France it has happened five times since 1814. A German, even when he has been beaten, has lived off other people's substance and saved his own.

It is impossible for the Germans to feel about war the way other Europeans do, because no matter what happens to make Germany dislike the memory of this war, war in the past has been too kind to her.

THE NEXT WAR

That is probably why the "best" Nazi minds of to-day are already preparing the next war.

Here are the conclusions of a report by General von Stuelpnagel written in February 1942, just after the first reverses in Russia and after America had been drawn into the war:

"What would a temporary defeat matter to us, if we obtain a margin of superiority over our neighbors, greater than the one we had before 1939, from an economic and demographic viewpoint, thanks to the destruction of manpower and of material which we have accumulated? If we obtain that margin, the war will have been useful, as we shall be able to resume it on military grounds in better conditions next time.

"The conquest of the world may demand many successive steps, but the essential thing is that after each step we should have an economical and mechanical potential that is stronger than that of the enemy.

"With the war chest amassed by us, the annihilation of human lives (two generations), the destruction of neighboring industries and what we can salvage of our own, we shall be in a better position to win in 25 years than we were in 1939. This maximum delay of 25 years is imperative as it is the period that Russia will need to repair what we have destroyed.

"The present war will be victorious in spite of temporary defeat since it will mean a step forward to power.

"We don't need to fear peace terms similar to those which we would impose, since our enemies will always be divided. We must try to sow the germs for such divisions in the next peace treaty. Our heroes are not dying in vain since they will leave a Germany wealthier and less weakened than the victors will be. We cannot conquer the world in one single war.

"Our enemies already admit that the 1920 slogan, 'Germany will pay' has no longer any meaning. We shall supply a few battalions of workers, we shall give back a few unsold works of art, some out-of-date machines, and we can always say that the things they claim were destroyed by their own bombings. There can be no proof to the contrary. . . . Then, time will do its work. Our enemies will get tired before we shall. Above all, a line of propaganda will have to be created to keep up the morale in our country and explain how this war ended in a victory in spite of military defeat, and that the next conflict will finally bring the accomplishment of our Germanic will to power. We must work for that aim from now on and not hesitate to organize a propaganda campaign calling for charity, in order to be supplied and fed as long as possible by our enemies.

"We must also keep control of the world production of raw materials needed for war, and we shall have to camouflage, for a time, the degree of control which we have attained. We must also preserve our deposits in foreign countries and we must see to it that no supervisory commission of the United Nations can discover them. These are the conditions of our next victory." [1]

Marshal von Rundstedt in his lectures at the Imperial War Academy of Berlin said:

"The total destruction of neighboring people and of their wealth is indispensable for our victory. One of our great mistakes in 1918 was to spare the lives of civilians in enemy countries. We should always be twice as numerous as the total population of nations which are contiguous to the Greater Reich. This means that we should destroy at least one third of the population in the neighboring countries: the only way is organized under-feeding. It is always better than the machine-gun as there are limits and inconveniences about killing. Famine can do better, especially with the young." [2]

[1] *Combat* (Algiers edition) Nov. 28, 1943.
[2] *Id.*

Another quotation from the *Voelkische Beobachter* of September 2, 1943, and still another from a circular by General von Mannstein of September 17th of the same year repeat the same general line. One last passage from the *Schwarze Korps*, October 14, says:

"Either Europe will be rebuilt, and it can be done only by us, or else there will be everlasting chaos and final ruin. Our interest is to make the war last as long as possible. The longer it lasts, the greater the heap of destruction, the more will economy and demography suffer,—and the loss of balance will be in our favor. The interest of Anglo-Saxon imperialism is to preserve its European market and to stop the annihilation of its clients. The Yankees' demand for a war to the finish is pure window-dressing, as their secret wish is for a peace of compromise with temporary political stop-gaps such as Darlan and Badoglio." [1]

The Algiers press from which we quote the passages above goes on to say:

"The Germans are hoping for a new Versailles Treaty so that they can soon get rid of the obligations imposed upon them.

"The amount of Nazi thefts in Europe, including Russia, has reached astronomical figures. It is valued at between 50 and 60 billion dollars. The war indemnities paid by Europe to Germany amount to 54 billion dollars to this day—Nov. 28, 1943, that is, 60 times more than Germany paid after the last war. These sums represent an enormous wealth accumulated by the Nazis in the form of booty; it is the future war chest and will enable them to resume their conquest of the world.

"These sums are deposited in banks of neutral coun-

[1] *Id.*

tries, Switzerland, Sweden, Spain, South American Republics and especially Argentina, in the name of native citizens or camouflaged corporations. These banks will try to keep these deposits for after-war financing of world reconstruction, enterprizes in Africa and the Pacific. These banks will bring every form of pressure to bear upon their governments so that no investigation takes place and the secret be maintained."

THE EUROPEAN SOLUTION

What then could be the terms of "a just and lasting peace" in regard to Germany, if the thieves keep the stolen goods, the aggressors find themselves "in a better position" for the next attack?

I do not pretend to have all the answers, but some common sense combined with the following propositions, neither new nor startling, seem to me to be prerequisites.

A victory should mean:
1. That the German war machine be destroyed in all its forms and never rebuilt.
2. That the hold of Prussia on the rest of Germany should be broken.
3. That German property, public and private, should account for the property stolen from the United Nations.
4. That all Germans, considered as individuals, should enjoy their full rights to "life, liberty and the pursuit of happiness," but should start that life again from scratch, not with the accumulated assets resulting from plunder and extortion.

On the destruction of German weapons and of the tools

to make them, there is no controversy. All the Allies and all their political parties want this physical elimination of the German war machine. The question raised by skeptics is: Can it be maintained through the years? Last time, Germany rearmed.

Last time, Germany rearmed after 15 years because nobody stopped her. The British signed a special treaty in 1935 authorizing Germany to acquire a navy equal to that of France. In America, people looked on with unconcern. I read articles saying that another of those impossible features of the Versailles Treaty was going by the board. The authors were unaware that German disarmament was also part of the Berlin Treaty of August 1921 between the United States and Germany, the separate treaty signed by President Harding, which was supposed to be pure from the wicked provisions signed by President Wilson at Versailles. When Hitler rearmed, it occurred to almost no American that Germany was openly violating a solemn, separate treaty with the United States. The American sentiment was: "The Allies get what they deserve." The same irresponsible attitude made possible the militarization of the Pacific islands under Japanese mandate.

Is it not probable that the American attitude will be different this time, especially when the Americans will have felt the full disturbing effect of the war on their economy? German disarmament can be enforced if Europe is determined to see it enforced. It was not made complete in 1919, because the Western Governments still had in mind the possible use of German force against Russia. This time, no such ideas will be permitted by European majority opinion.

Concerning Prussia, it seems that too much emphasis

has been put on a utopian "dismemberment" of Germany, extremely difficult to maintain against the natural wish of the Germans to unite again; and not enough attention has been given to breaking up the Prussian hold on the rest of Germany, thereby provoking a normal decentralization of the whole country. Such a move, directed against Berlin as usurper of all German authority, would have deep historical justification. Instead of an artificial gesture destined to hurt Germany, imposed entirely from the outside and calculated to exasperate every German good or bad, an anti-Prussian policy might be largely engineered through the will for self-government, peace, and a return to happier traditions, on the part of Bavarians, Saxons, Rhinelanders, Hanoverians, Württembergers and citizens of the old free cities of Hamburg, Bremen and Lübeck. All these have a long, rich history, where Prussia played no part, or up to 1871 played the part of an enemy. Heinrich Heine's writings of 100 years ago should be re-read, especially *Deutschland, ein Wintermaerchen,* where he shows his dismay at the encroachments of Prussian bureaucracy and militarism, the spread of the spike-helmet, and the slow deterioration of the old German civilization under the impact of the new "efficiency."

For a century, the Germans laughed when a foreigner criticized this Prussification. They liked it because it was successful. But now that it has brought them disaster, not only the cultural disaster deplored by Heine, but military defeat twice and this time invasion and destruction, perhaps the Germans will reconsider the wisdom of following Prussian leadership and espousing Prussian aims. The Prussians, whose blood is scarcely German and who were long regarded as foreigners this side of Brandenburg, have been the conquerors of modern Germany and its curse. Even the valid and heroic side of their Spartan ethics and feudal traditions do not fit into this modern world, which calls for other forms of courage and devotion. Prussia played the part of evil genius to the 19th century. The words attributed to Blücher when he visited London after Waterloo and contemplated the vast city from a high point, are, "Gott, was fur Plunder!" Those words still summarize the aspirations of the present-day German generals.

Europe of 100 years ago was ready for peace, and it is a fact that European writers of the 30s, 40s and 50s regarded the era of great wars as being over with Napoleon. War, they said, did not pay. Then came Bismarck and the campaigns of 1864 against Denmark, 1866 against Austria and 1870 against France, proving that war could still pay. Then Europe relapsed into militarism, all the nations of the world went to the German school, and peace and civilization were thrown back a century. That was the gift of Prussia to Europe.

I believe that a great deal of German support could be enlisted to liberate Germany and Europe from the curse of Prussianism. And it will make a great deal of difference if we carry out a policy based on ancient and authentic German trends and traditions, connected with German periods of *real* greatness, rather than improvise a policy which no German can genuinely subscribe to. Moreover, the policy of forceful dismemberment shows a fear of Germany which can only make the Germans wish to be fear-inspiring again. As I said before, either we fail to build up a healthy Europe, in which case the Germans will remain dangerous whatever we do to them; or we succeed, and need not fear Germany, united or not, because we organized Europeans shall be in a proportion of six to one to the Germans.

NATURE OF THE GUILT

Our third point, concerning the confiscation of German property, is likely to arouse numerous objections. We shall try, at least, to make our point clear.

Let us notice first that German proletarians, who at the close of the war will be probably 95% of the German people, have nothing to lose. Are we going to feel such respect for the property of the remaining 5%, that we do not dare to confiscate it, as a partial repayment for five years of international plundering, and as a reminder that war's balance sheet does not *always* resolve itself into a profit?

The juridical basis for this restitution of stolen goods is an extremely simple one. There is no need to invoke the personal guilt of each German in every atrocity that was committed. Let it suffice to call every German property-owner guilty of *association with a crook*.

He knew who Hitler was. He knew what the Nazis were driving at, and by what methods. He would have gladly shared the profits, had Hitler been successful. There is not a shadow of a sign that German property owners disapproved of Hitler's enterprises, nor that they would have declined to receive their share of the plunder. What is the least to be exacted if a man has been knowingly the partner of a crook and the crook has been found out? Is the partner allowed to go on, undisturbed?

The total loss of one's property is far from being the most cruel thing that can happen. There are many people in prosperous countries who cannot conceive of anything more terrible. But the Europeans who have witnessed the massacre of Jews, the killing of hostages, the wholesale deportation of Poles, the methodical starving of children—those Europeans may find that such a solution of the German problem is not too harsh.

As for the German proletarian, I am not sure that he will not approve this confiscation. He has been ruined and betrayed by the Nazis for the benefit of a few. I doubt if he will rise in the defense of those few, when the day of reckoning comes.

The German proletarian, workman or farmer, and the German young man of tomorrow, should feel that the future is wide open and that there is no tribute, no humiliation in perspective. What they earn honestly, they will keep. The whole tribute should be paid at once by those who speculated on a Nazi victory. Their investment was worthless. Let them know it as soon, as clearly and as totally as possible.

I insist that this operation is simpler, more equitable and more impressive than the imposition of a slow tribute, to be paid over a long period of years. For instance, if a German liberal who fought Hitler, who had to abandon all his possessions and emigrate, should return to his country after this war and make good in his profession, he will have to pay a substantial contribution to the reparations to come—which is unjust. A Nazi official who stole from foreigners and from his countrymen, who has acquired a comfortable establishment, some land and some safe capital as a result, and settles down after the war to enjoy the profits of his plundering, will go practically undisturbed. That is unjust too. To him and to the like of him, the war will have proved an excellent operation. His sons will have all the moral preparation needed for a Third German War. Why shouldn't they look forward to it with complacency?

As to the administration of that former German estate, constituted by public property and by all private property above a certain level, it does not seem too difficult to devise a European board of trusteeship. There is no question of dispossessing the proletarians of their belongings, nor anyone of his instruments of work or personal and family objects. Let us add that over a long period, an option should be given to the Germans for redeeming these possessions, public or private. Buying back their railroads or their museums, their estates or their factories, should be facilitated by liberal provisions. But I submit that all present German property being the equivalent of stolen property, it is both a scandal and a danger that Germans should retain the ownership of their estates, railroads, factories, museums, shipyards and stores, whereas dispossessed Poles, Greeks, Norwegians and Czechs will return from exile or forced labor to find *their* property gone, because the Germans had been living on it all these years.

Anyway, the important distinction to make is not between the good and the bad Germans. It is between Germans of to-day, who followed Hitler, and Germans of to-morrow. This is where the wedge should be driven.

Exoneration of to-day's Germans is an encouragement to relapse into more aggressions, under new leaders.

Burdens and penalties imposed on the Germans of the future will naturally engender rebellion, open or not, and a wish to overthrow the world's order.

The trouble is that the mentality of "normal" business

has pervaded our Western thinking to such an extent that spreading reparations over a long period of years seems to most people like a normal banking operation, instead of the monstrosity it is: forgiving the criminals and placing the penalty on their children and grandchildren, yet to be born.

I have no illusion.

These simple suggestions will not be adopted, the wealthy Germans will get away with their secret deposits abroad, the Prussian officers will assemble again, the workmen will toil to pay by instalments, and will hate the world for it. Economists will explain that German Economy should not be "disrupted," industrialists will feel a vague sense of solidarity with the poor rich Germans who were unlucky with their investments, and people throughout the world will prefer to forget.

FRANCE

FRANCE IN EUROPE

ON AUGUST 26, 1944, THE NEW YORK POST PUBLISHED AN article by Edgar A. Mowrer on the liberation of Paris. Its conclusion was the following:

"With the liberation of Paris, Europe has found a voice. Who else could speak for the continent? Not the Pope, for his church claims universality. Not all-too-lately Fascist Rome. Not the neutrals—they are too small. Not unhappy Madrid, writhing under its tyrant. Not Berlin—traitor to Europe and to mankind.

"But in Paris, Europe has again found a voice. This writer will not be surprised if the voice of Europe turns out to be more strident than Washington, London and Moscow have anticipated."

Thus did the unreal situation come to an end, during which France "was no more" as certain commentators put it. Things are resuming their true shape. France is the largest of the ten "resisting" nations which are, in my opinion, the backbone of the new Europe. Therefore Mowrer is right: Paris can speak for the largest group of nations and of people in the Western World.

To the patriotic impulse that motivated the French in their fight for liberation, another is to be added. It may not be quite articulate with every man, yet it is there. It is the idea that peace will prevail in Europe when there will be a Europe. The idea of building a healthy and peaceful Europe by collective effort has ancient roots in France. It was expressed by Henry IV, by Victor Hugo, by Aristide Briand and many others, and endorsed by popular approval, but in a sort of ineffectual and platonic manner. Now it has come to the forefront, as a condition for the continued existence of France and of her sister nations on the Continent.

The idea was stolen by Hitler, along with many other things, and was put forward by him because of its sure appeal to many millions. Had Hitler, after Munich, extolled the idea of European Union and made it come true under German leadership, no one would have known how to oppose it. But today, no European believes that Hitler's New Europe could have fulfilled our long and reasonable hopes. His was not even a step in the right direction. And this is one more reason why men fight him: to retake possession of an idea which he kidnapped and disfigured.

Some Free French fighters did not think any further than the liberation of France. Yet from letters, from publications in London, the underground press and elsewhere, we see that many among the most militant had not given up the idea of an efficient world organization after this war. They shared this hope with their British friends. Is there any reason why Frenchmen, who were leading before 1935, in regard to a European Union, should be far behind today? A number of my friends, who worked with me for the realistic idea of a collective enforcement of peace, are among the leaders of the Free French.

Ideas of collective security that used to be French are now being adopted by public opinion in the United Nations. This is no time for the French to repudiate them.

In 1918, when the French infantryman came home from spending four years in the trenches, his first thought was: "And now, *anything* so that my kids, when they grow up, won't have to go through this as I did."

This was no statesman's conception. It was the creed of "Jacques Bonhomme."

He went further than forming a wish. He figured it all out, like this—"War is stupid, dirty, cruel, ruinous and obsolete. It's bad enough to win a war. But surely no nation would wage war if she were *sure* to lose it? Well, no nation can possibly win against a coalition of all the others. Even Napoleon could not. So if all are determined to break the back of any war-maker, *and if they say so, clearly, in advance,* nobody is going to try. If we stay separate and can be attacked one by one, somebody is bound to try again . . . What we need is a world society with a big stick; and then the problem is solved."

Today the novelty is *not* the resurgence of that ultra-simple notion that "we must hang together, or else we shall hang separately." The novelty is that the great American nation and the great Russian nation, the two most powerful units in the world today, are with us this time.

If such is the case, we, the French, in spite of everything, have not exhausted our capacity for hope.

The will for national independence exists throughout the world. What characterizes the French attitude is that because of their attachment to *personal* rights, their service to national independence makes fighting for French liberties and fighting for universal human rights, practically one and the same.

Throughout their long history, the French, like other

nations, have fought, or been ready to fight, for the independence of their country.

Little children know about the people repelling Attila and the Huns fifteen hundred years ago. They know about the Parisians resisting the Northmen who rowed their boats up the Seine, in the 9th Century. They have heard about the fifty invasions which the country suffered. To the foreign conqueror, be he German or British or Spanish or Saracen, the people said *no*.

Against internal oppression, too, the people have had a long training in saying *no*. Feudal tyranny or religious intolerance finally disappeared because of so many generations of French people who said *no*.

In the recent German conquest all forms of oppression were combined; foreign occupation, economic exploitation, spiritual tyranny. As a result, all the motives for resistance merged into the Free French cause. Every man who said *no* to the German victory, as early as June 1940, was a Free Frenchman at heart, whether his motive was national or personal, patriotic or philosophical, or just a reflex.

PERSONAL FREEDOM AND NATIONAL UNITY

The French people are among those who have lived most thoroughly and most intensely with liberty. That is a word which had become moldy with misuse, and has been scrubbed clean by misfortune, oppression and revolt.

The freedom of the French is open to constant misinterpretation. That France is a land of pleasant laissez-faire, of libertine enjoyment is true, but that its spiritual discipline is of the strictest order is also true. Studies are arduous, professions exacting and honor is often a tyrant. The France of Corneille, of Pascal and of Péguy, is hardly the world's playground.

Does one realize how much of the internal disputes among the French are the price of their very love for freedom? People who live like sheep have no inner conflicts. They are incapable of diversity. French divergent opinions will not disappear, because they are rooted deeply in powerful convictions. The important question is, what form will opposition take?

The French are far from being unable to live side by side, at peace, in spite of their differences. Remember that from 1871 to 1934, through 63 years there was no serious internal fighting in France. And yet, people did quarrel! They lived through the difficult first years of the Third Republic, the Dreyfus trials, the Separation of Church and State, the rise of labor parties, the war of 1914–1918, the economic crises that followed. If one took seriously the headlines of some newspapers, they were each week on the brink of civil war. But if a nation resists for 63 years the temptations of civil war, it shows that it has powerful brakes; it shows that reason intervenes to stop violence.

The truth of the matter is that there are other ways of salvation for France than to aspire toward what could only be an artificial and insincere unity of spirit.

Listen to Renan when he addressed in September 1871 the German David Strauss: "For my part, I would resent a world where all men led the same life that I lead . . . I have personally enforced the strict observance of rules of morals, as a former member of the Church; but I would be sorry if there were not worldly people to represent a freer life . . . I am not a Catholic; but I am very glad there are

Catholics, Sisters of Charity, country priests, Carmelites, and if I had it in my power to suppress it all, I would not do it."

If the French became all alike, their role in the world would be at an end. For the French are the guardians of the diversity of the world. Without the French, the world would run the risk of sliding into uniformity. Look at the regimes that almost won the war.

Not only do Frenchmen differ but everyone of them is the bearer of diversity within himself. If he loves liberty so much, it is because liberty is the condition of this diversity. Every Frenchman would willingly build up his own universe, entirely by hand. They all do not succeed in this venture, but they all make a point of trying.

The whole problem of democracy is establishing an order that protects everyone's freedom. If you reduce democracy to the bare notion of sovereignty by numbers, democracy runs the risk of grossly opposing civilization; Montesquieu and Jefferson were well aware of this. The French sentiment on this is: Yes, the majority decides, because someone must necessarily decide; but the majority is not necessarily right. I am the one who is right, because I defend my principles. You too are right, because you defend yours. The majority is the umpire and we accept its decision, because otherwise there would be anarchy. But that does not mean that you change your mind. You only change your mind if and when you have been convinced. In France there are no "landslides," no "bandwagons." And so we shall live side by side, you with your ideas and I with mine. The majority is not going to try and wrest them away, because we won't try to rise against it. There exists that contract between law on the one hand, and the individual on the other hand. And that to us is a civilized state.

The very prerequisite of a high-grade civilization is not to look upon violence as an instrument of persuasion.

There remain in France about half a dozen deeply rooted convictions that would seem contradictory. But each has slowly ripened, in close companionship with the others, exchanging with them sap or fragrance. No one of these tendencies, half-spiritual, half-political, could alone represent France. Should we expect them to destroy one another? It would be a relapse into the era of religious wars.

How is French unity possible then? Only through a process of free choice, wherein members of all groups and creeds choose to be French first and last, where allegiance to one party or another gives way before the superior allegiance to France herself.

There is a French history yet to be written, which would describe the local rebellions of provinces refusing to belong to a foreign master. Auvergne against the Romans, Normandy against the English, Flanders against the Spaniards, Provence against the Saracens. All are accustomed to fighting for independence. This war is merely the last one in a long series.

Hitler did not unify France; that was done long ago. But he reminded the French that they were one people, regardless of party, class, race or climate. It evokes that other war of independence, 165 years ago, when Virginians, New Englanders, Carolinians, Pennsylvanians and New Yorkers fought for their rights.

The deep resemblance lies in that free decision of men whom nobody coerced into action. Elsewhere, a leader comes, he is followed, and he orders what the people should believe. First the leader, then the creed. With the Continental army and with the Maquis, on the contrary, first grows the creed, then the leaders who are accepted because they incarnate the creed. This is essential and explains much of the misunderstandings about France.

Since 1940 we have heard people, including France's faithful friends, wondering what kind of leadership fate had in store for the French. The answer is: France makes her leaders herself. She made de Gaulle because she needed him. France did not change herself to suit him, as nations do under a dictator. The man became what France demanded that he should be. We know that he was constantly preoccupied to the point of torment with what France expected him to do, or to be.

Once in a while in history, France knows what she wants and she knows what she hates. Then France stands like one individual and everything concerning her becomes so simple, so crystal-clear, that observers no longer see the usual mosaic of conflicting allegiances, provinces, interests, races, tastes, and climates. Then France is no longer the many-sided, she has but one voice, one will, one idea. Yesterday it was liberation. Today it is reconstruction.

THE QUEST FOR MAN

What does France stand for, that makes her irreplaceable? Many answers have been given, and we propose to add one more:

France is the land where the quest of man for knowledge of his own self and for possession of his own fate has been pursued most ardently. The French are the people who most continuously regard living, the science or the art or the pleasure or the burden of living, as the most important of all occupations. What may have confused many observers is that this quest can take such a variety of forms, from the highest spiritual endeavor to the most tangible and hedonistic of pursuits.

Therefore, even when defeated, the French withdraw to positions prepared one thousand years in advance. That is, inside themselves, where no conqueror can reach.

Every Frenchman insists on his own interpretation of what his honor requires. It is like a religion kept by everyone without any need for priesthood or proselytism.

A Frenchman is at his best in the individual professions, enterprises, arts and sports. France is a mother of inventors and of critics, of pioneers and of historians, all that requires and brings out personal independence of action or judgment. Therefore, further contributions from French thinking are needed in a world where collective efficiency and mass thinking are more and more dangerously prevalent.

This is summed up by what John Erskine expressed in a remarkable address a few months ago:

"The first thing that Americans admire in France is adventurous thinking.... In France today, among the boys and girls growing up in hovels, there are some who will give us ideas for which later Jeffersons will say 'thank you.'" [1]

I don't know whether the French were right or wrong when they forged for themselves that particular culture, based on man. But there is no sign whatever that they will abandon or repudiate it.

[1] French American Club of New York, June 4, 1942.

Yes, individualism has cost France a great deal, but it has saved her, too. That need for personal autonomy, that capacity for individual resistance made things difficult indeed for our leaders, throughout history; but it also made impossible the task of our conquerors.

The French need not look far for examples of a refusal to submit to outside authority, when it is imposed without their consent. Both their history and their literature glorify it.

The example indeed comes from France herself: each time events ordered that she should disappear, she refused to obey.

FRENCH POLICIES

Let us now examine, very briefly since future events will obviously influence it, the probable behavior of the French Republic in its internal and foreign policies.

I will venture the following propositions:

1. No landslide giving control to any extremist party will take place in the near future. Extremists to the right have been discredited, by their complacency to say the least toward the Fascist dictators. As for the Communists, whose courage and discipline in the Underground work and fighting have compelled admiration and respect, they are a minority, probably less than 15% in the whole country, and the memory of the deal between Stalin and Hitler is too recent to let the French forget that cases may arise when communists will be communists first, and French only second. Subservience to orders from Rome was the great popular grudge against the Catholic priesthood throughout the 19th century. Subservience to Moscow discipline is likely to produce the same reaction.

2. This being said, there is no reason to expect that the alignment of party ideologies in the last regular elections, those of 1936, will be substantially modified, except for a further weakening of the Right. The liberal Christian parties (Démocrates Populaires, Socialistes Chrétiens, etc.) will probably be strengthened, due to the continuity of their record, and their constructive contribution to national and international thinking. The socialists, who had 25% of the seats in Parliament, will probably retain as many if not gain more, and find themselves, as in 1936, very close to the middle-of-the-road within the majority. Therefore it may be expected that the political center of gravity of parliament and of the country will be somewhere among the moderate socialists. This fact is the more interesting, since a similar situation exists in most of the ten countries we have considered as forming the backbone of tomorrow's Europe.[1]

3. The ideas of Aristide Briand on foreign policy, which were scandalously misrepresented in most of the French press but were endorsed by a substantial majority of the French people, have been vindicated by events. The need for collective security, an effective enforcement of peace to precede and make possible a reduction of armaments, for some definite federal ties between the nations of Europe, all these simple notions, which most of our plain people understood so well but which puzzled the more sophisticated classes, have now passed from utopia into reality.

[1] Many French Leftists would endorse Oscar Wilde's statement written half a century ago in *The Soul of Man under Socialism:* "Socialism will be of value simply because it will lead to Individualism . . . if we are to have Industrial Tyrannies, then the last state of man will be worse than the first . . . it is clear that no Authoritarian Socialism will do."

4. While wishing for, and contributing to, the creation of a world society which will be universal in its scope, but for which some nations are definitely not ready, the French will look around them for a way of effecting an immediate enforcement of peace and order on their continent. Their regional policy of security will lead to close collaboration first with their neighbors, England and the free nations of Western Europe, then with Russia and the free nations of Central and Eastern Europe. France has everything to gain and nothing to lose in supporting, to the utmost of her capacity, the European system which has been outlined in the early chapters of this book.

5. France will *not* fall into any single "sphere of influence," nor will she try to barricade herself and her clients in a water-tight "sphere of influence" of her own. Each large nation radiates influence. But such influences are overlapping. France is in no mood to renounce her close ties and mutual exchanges, and those which are to come, with England, with the United States or with Russia, in order to "belong" in a special circle with either of these great friendly powers. What we say for France applies also to Czechoslovakia, to Belgium, to Greece. I believe that everyone of the liberated nations will insist, as France will, for a *balance of friendship* (to replace the old balance of power—and of distrust), between all of the leading world powers.[1]

[1] The bulletin "Free France," published by the French Press and Information Service in New York, contained the following in its October 15, 1944, issue:

FRANCE IN THE EUROPE OF TOMORROW

This is the title of Chapter IV of the review Les Cahiers Politiques, *published secretly by the Resistance. It was founded by a Resistance group of scholars including François de Menthon, Commissioner of Justice, René Courtain, Secretary-General for National Economy, and*

As to France's attitude toward the great world schemes of today, it is expressed in this passage from the French note on the proposed amendments to the Dumbarton Oaks plan (April 1945): "France would be ready to commit herself even further than the Dumbarton Oaks plan and to consent to greater limitations of sovereignty, in exchange for a better international organization."

FROM EMPIRE TO FEDERATION

An important feature of the new times, calling for "new eyes" to appraise it, is the change in relations between European countries and their overseas "empires."

Together with the mother country, the French empire has some 112 million inhabitants. It comes fifth among the

---

Henri Teitgen, Commissioner of Information—all young men, all sincere republicans, all convinced of the necessity for just and responsible international cooperation.

... "France is more likely than anyone else to state the principles upon which may be based a European order in liberty and peace. More than anyone else is she able to work for the creation of a United States of Europe, and her misfortunes will, more effectively than any promises, place her above the accusation of imperialism. The union of France and the other liberated countries will be for France as for the others the best guarantee against any outside supervision of the Continent, in preventing which France and the others are equally interested. Even the vanquished will have a place in this union, although it would be unwise to attempt today to state their place in detail.

Such a union in no way implies any sort of hostility to America, and still less to Russia. We even believe that French initiative in the creation of a federated Europe would provide all necessary guarantees for Russia, first in warding off the domination of any plutocracy over the Continent, second in establishing on Russia's western frontiers a true peace in accordance with the facts of history and the desires of the populations. The objective of federation is to make certain that Europe will not become the jousting ground and locale of a struggle between rival influences, and this objective should cause concern to no one."

(*Les Cahiers Politiques*, n 5, January, 1944.)

largest national groups on earth: only the British Empire, China, the Soviet Union and United States have a larger population.

What many of us have discovered only lately is that this French empire *is* a close unit. Strangely enough, the objective demonstration of this fact was provided by defeat itself. In 1940, continental France was invaded, a semi-puppet government was set up under protection of enemy bayonets, and French prestige was at its lowest level in centuries. Nothing was easier at that time, than for French possessions overseas to cut loose from France and either proclaim independence or join other national units. If they had wanted to, no force could have prevented them from doing so. What happened, on the contrary, was that in the French territories overseas the national resistance was reborn and organized. For two years Brazzaville became the capital of what was left of a free French commonwealth. The will to fight and maintain French nationality came from the natives themselves, who had some idea of what totalitarian rule would mean for colonial populations. Governor Eboué of Equatorial Africa, a full-blooded African, gave extremely pertinent expression to the native point of view, while the famous "colonne Leclerc" which started from the heart of Africa, struck across the Tchad and the Sahara and fell on Rommel's flank at Tripoli, was mostly composed of African troops.[1]

The reason for this situation is to be found in the fundamental French theory of colonization, which holds good

[1] The other colonies showed the same spirit. Wherever Vichy remained in authority, as in Martinique, volunteers escaped in large numbers to join the Free French forces. Indo-China, under Japanese control and far from any Allied support, most certainly feels the same way, as we shall see when the time comes.

in spite of the many mistakes that have been made. That colonization, which goes back to Coligny and Henry IV in the 16th Century, is agrarian in its essence, and based on race equality. It found its vindication during these dangerous years. Therefore, if there had been any doubts as to the inherent rights of natives to Empire citizenship, these doubts are dispelled. Only qualifications of education and civic training, not of color, will be taken into consideration for the exercise of these rights. That is the meaning of the new policies outlined in 1943 by the French Commissioner for Colonies, René Pleven, at the Consultative Assembly in Algiers.[1]

I have dwelt on the particular case of France, not only because I know it better than others, but because of what Mowrer expressed in the passage quoted before. The voice of France may be the voice of Europe. In the meetings of the governments in exile in London, during this war, the French language remained the official medium. Of the ten liberated countries on the Continent, at least seven are more likely to use French than English, at international conferences.[2] This does not call for any privileges or special rights to be claimed by France. It happens that she finds herself once more in a central position among her sister nations, and that she is far more conscious of it than she was after her victory in 1918.

[1] Cf. French Press and Information publications, especially the recent pamphlet entitled "Toward a Federal Union—the French Solution of the Colonial Problem." Also *Foreign Affairs*, October, 1944, the article by Governor P. O. Lapie.
[2] At the Assembly of the League of Nations where English and French were the two official languages, approximately 40 delegations used French and 10 used English.

Our solidarity with the other 100 million Europeans who suffered as the French suffered, resisted as the French resisted, and hoped as the French hoped, is more than a passing phase. They can speak for us and we can speak for them. We need their liberation as they needed ours. If there is to be security and happiness in Europe, it must be for all her free men. That is what we will say when we speak to the world in her name.

REPUBLIC VERSUS EMPIRE

THE "GREAT DESIGN"

THE PRESENT WAR WILL BE DEFINED BY HISTORY AS THE final climax in the long conflict of two ideas—world empire and world republic.

Europe has been the chief theatre of that conflict. The Roman Empire, the Moslem Empire, that of Charles V, and that of Napoleon, were partial realizations of an imperial scheme of total domination. Because of the combined efforts of other powers, it has always failed.

The alternate idea, based on a federation where each nation should retain its right to existence, appeared in the late Middle Ages and made slow progress during the last six hundred years in the conscience of the European people.

Henry IV of France drafted such a plan between 1600 and 1610, and died as it was about to materialize.

Henry IV laid the foundations of his "great scheme" of European union, immediately after the Peace of Vervins (1598) which terminated his war of liberation from the Spaniards. That same year, he had promulgated the famous Edict of Nantes, granting religious freedom to the Huguenots and putting an end to the long religious wars of the 16th century.

The "great scheme" proceeded from a very simple idea, but its realization implied many successive steps. The

King began with those most immediately feasible. The intent was fourfold: to check the ambitions of the Germanic Empire, which had threatened to engulf all Europe under Charles V; to form a united Christian Europe capable of resisting the Moslem invaders (80 years later the Turks were to lay siege before Vienna); to give peace, tranquillity and religious freedom to the peoples of Europe, who had suffered from too many wars; and finally to ensure France's position, prestige and security, by other means than the subjugation of other nations.

Henry's mind was both liberal and realistic. He conceived a vast alliance, federation or "republic" of all Christian nations, who would *keep* their respective sovereignties and keep the peace among themselves by solving their disputes through a supreme European council. It would be futile to discuss whether his chief motive was Christian zeal, love of glory, or the service of France, because the same foreign policy might have been dictated by either of these motives, and probably was by all three.

The alliance excluded no one. Both Catholic and Protestant States were expected to join. But as the Imperial foreign policy was in direct opposition to the scheme, it had first to take the shape of a coalition against the House of Austria. After ten years of negotiations, a European entente was realized, which included England, the Low Countries, the Scandinavians, the Protestant princes in Germany, Bohemia and Hungary, the Pope, Venice, Tuscany, the Swiss Cantons, Savoy, and the oppressed subjects of King Philip II of Spain, such as the Navarrese and the Morisques of Valencia.

This was no ordinary diplomatic combine. It was, potentially, an international force, and the realistic foundation of a League of Nations capable of enforcing peace. The various allies could supply 140,000 soldiers, and France 100,000. That was more than any single dissenting State could muster against the coalition.

There was no attempt at intrusion into the internal affairs of member nations, and no attempt to unify their extremely varied forms of government. The pragmatic temperament of Henry IV preserved him from such utopian endeavors. The essential purpose was to assemble fifteen Christian "dominions":

Six hereditary monarchies: France, Spain, England, Denmark, Sweden, Savoy.

Six elective sovereignties: the Papacy, the Empire, Poland, Hungary, Bohemia and Venice.

Three republics: the Netherlands, Switzerland, and the Italian confederation, which was to include the free cities of Genoa, Pisa, Florence, Mantua, Modena, Parma, etc.

We shall not go into the details of how the European Council was to adjust disputes and enforce its decisions. It implied, of course, the acceptance of a super-State, yet maintained the sovereign rights of each State, except the right to use war as an instrument of national policy.

Henry IV was assassinated in 1610. The idea was abandoned, and not revived till the Holy Alliance of 1815, which was less universal and less liberal. In the meantime, Europe suffered interminable wars, and even through the 19th and the early 20th century, down to the Briand proposals of 1929, there was not a single ruler, king, emperor or prime minister, who had enough imagination and enough courage to revive the "great scheme." Philosophers like Kant and poets like Hugo thought and wrote about it, and many students of history, no doubt, dreamt of it, but statesmen had, evidently, more important business to attend to.

The French Revolution offered the idea of a European federation of democratic peoples, and the Holy Alliance of 1815 retained the idea of federation, but dropped "democracy."

Napoleon is the only man in history who represented in succession the two principles of a republican federation and of imperial unity. He came to embody the principle of universal domination, while his enemies and his own troops still regarded him as a champion of universal revolution. His fortune was built upon a misunderstanding. Europe was presented with order, reason, logic, equal rights, efficient government and strict discipline, when its people had just begun to expect an entirely different gift —that thing called freedom.

Once he had dropped the revolutionary message, Napoleon ceased to be universal. He became only imperial. Beethoven and Goethe both realized it.

During the First World War, the will to world organization was formulated almost simultaneously by Woodrow Wilson and by the Soviets. The League of Nations and the Third Internationale were the only two rival world propositions between which people could choose. Most people refused the second and did not know much about the first.

The problem still presented itself in the old form: "nationalism" versus "internationalism." The "patriots" were aligned on one side and the "pacifists" on the other. Some people, like myself, struggled for twenty years against this fictitious alignment, but we were too few and far apart. We tried to show that most pacifists were ruining the cause of peace by attacking patriotism, which they could not destroy anyway, while most patriots were preparing the ruin of their own country, by refusing to support an international enforcement of order.

In our time, common sense statesmanship almost succeeded in establishing Europe. The victors of World War I accomplished only half of the job. They freed 55 million Europeans from foreign rule, and drew boundaries that were better than those of any similar settlement in history. But then the victors left the nations of Europe to shift for themselves behind their frontiers without any common plan, without consciousness of their common interest, without common leadership of any kind.

Each nation, filled with a sense of its sovereignty, but lacking a sense of European responsibility and foresight, drew on the immediate profits of independence, and neglected the future advantages of co-operation.

The frontiers, as such, were not to blame, but the use made of them to choke trade and to protect unhealthy industries was very much to blame. For ten years, Europe lived within restricted horizons. Then a French statesman tried to apply to the whole continent the rules of common sense which had proved successful for the American continent. In 1929, Aristide Briand took the initiative and suggested a federation of the States of Europe.

There was barely time enough before the financial crisis broke out in America to consult all the governments of Europe and to receive their answers. Stresemann died that same year. The economic depression spread over the whole world. The following year when Germany felt the impact her morale was shattered. The first large wave of nazi representatives entered the Reichstag in September

1930; sad times had begun for Europe. Less than two years later, Briand died, and with him died many hopes, some vague and remote, and others most realistic, hopes based on that European unity of which he had been a political sponsor.

There was nothing utopian in the scheme. Profits were certain and sure to come for all of us. Some countries, Germany for one, would have profited more than others. Why not, provided everybody gain? Those who would have gained most were the nations of Central Europe, the very nations which the Versailles peace had most profoundly transformed without however supplying them with a positive, joint economy.

Instead of these unlimited possibilities, the crash of 1929 disrupted everything, everywhere. As a direct consequence, came Hitler, who "set the clock back" and confronted Europe with the old threat of Empire—in other words, German plunder and German power.

Three years after Briand's death, Germany went back to the old ways of brutality, of lying, of stealing. And all she found to oppose her was a Europe without a backbone, and with a negative consciousness of its interests and perils which did not go beyond "appeasement."

In contrast to Hitler's proposed world empire, no world republic has as yet materialized, except in a military sense. The United Nations know by this time that like Napoleon's opponents, they did have to stay banded together in order to win the war. But they are still talking about staying banded together to win the peace as if it were a very new and bold idea, which only the brave and the optimistic dare to tackle. The world is driven to unity by the sheer force of events. But the consciousness of that unity has barely started in the minds of a fraction of the human race. With the rest, it is still to be born.

In Europe, it is a different story. A majority of Europeans want Europe to be a close and efficient concern. For them the war was fought between, on one side, the European Empire, materialized in the Gestapo, the stormtroopers, the quisling police, and on the other, the European Republic.

The Empire would have destroyed their nations. The Republic may be the only way to preserve them against a perilous future. Thus the present victory of the European idea is a victory of patriotism.

NATIONALISM ALIVE

To understand this European evolution (which makes untenable the positions of both "antipatriot" and "antipacifist" of the old schools) we must keep in mind this fact which explains all the rest: this war is a War of Independence for Europe.

Most people in most countries know what this means. In almost every land, children, even before they are old enough to go to school, hear their parents talking about the dates, the events, the heroes of the wars for independence. In America, 1776. In Switzerland, William Tell. In France, Jeanne d'Arc, the volunteers of 1792, and the Marne. In England the defeat of the Spanish Armada. In Russia, Napoleon's invasion. There is no national controversy about these. Controversy flares up about the form of government, the distribution of wealth, domestic or foreign policy. About independence, there is no dissent.

When the Balkan nations declared war against Turkey in 1912, there was a general misunderstanding. The world looked for every motive except the simple one, understood by every illiterate peasant of Serbia, Greece or Bulgaria in the same terms as it was understood by their educated classes and their leaders. "We fight to set our brothers free." These brothers were the millions of Serbs, Greeks, and Bulgarians who lived under Turkish rule against their will.

These people, after centuries of this rule, were not resigned. They wanted their freedom, and they got it. The same thing happened a few years later to the millions of Czechs, Poles, Yugoslavs, Rumanians and others who were set free by World War I. In 1918, I addressed at Johnstown, Pennsylvania, an open-air meeting of 1200 Serbs from Austria-Hungary, recent immigrants who had found good jobs here. These 1200 men had just enlisted in the Serbian army and were about to sail as volunteers, knowing that if taken prisoner by the Austrians they would be hanged. They abandoned a profitable life in the land of their choice in order to risk their lives. Why?— "To set our brothers free."

There was not the remotest way of explaining their conduct through economic motives. Yet calling that action "sacrifice" is not entirely adequate either. These men were pleased to go, to do the right thing, to be together, to bring about what their fathers and forefathers had prayed for, to be the ones to fulfill the hope that is voiced in their ancient popular songs.

The motive for a war of independence is so simple that many observers lose sight of it. It is so transparent that one does not see it.

"Those people are in our cities, in our fields, in our homes. They were not invited. They must go."

There must be something fundamental, biological, ineradicable in this reaction to oppression. It occurs in all latitudes, and at all stages of civilization. The most highly cultured, internationally civilized individual feels it, when his country loses its freedom. The primitive man feels it when his miserable village is threatened by an enemy. It is not reasonable and it is not unreasonable. It has to do, not with thinking or willing, but with being.

Patriotism is not a product of reason. It belongs to the realm of feeling. Arguing for or against it does not affect its deep reality.

Love has a logic of its own. There is no use in looking for economic or utilitarian motives to explain the actions of a person who loves. A man may sacrifice his fortune or his career for a woman, and never regret it. A mother will give up everything for her child. All these things are neither exceptional nor monstrous. They happen every day. There are probably three people out of four who would be capable of risking their lives or their possessions for something or somebody, for an idea or a person.

Today national allegiance makes millions of men ready to throw away their comfort, their safety, their happiness, at a moment's notice. Political parties wear themselves out rapidly, but patriotism remains as vigorous as ever because it is an instinct. It is still the most formidable motive that can drive masses all over the world to the greatest sacrifices.

Causes and interests that endure are the ones that are rooted somewhere deeper than in circumstances or in the ability of a leader.

One of the Fascist poisons, flattering to the immature and habit-forming to the lazy, was in replacing reasoned, forceful allegiance to an idea, by blind worship for a man. Take away the leader and his popularity, and Fascism collapses. Take away the leader, and a war of independence keeps its full meaning, the cause, its full appeal.

This is because the roots of such a cause are not in momentary political or personal interests. A war of independence has its roots in deep soil. History records many wars of independence which were started and fought by numbers and with weapons ridiculously small and inadequate; any tabulation of forces at the time would have shown as hopeless the cause of George Washington, the cause of Bolivar, the cause of Karageorge or Botzaris or Garibaldi or Paderewski, or Masaryk. Each of them was, at first, regarded as the negligible leader of a contemptible little rebellion. Yet every one of these rebellions against large and powerful empires ended in victory.

There is one way, and only one, to silence that hunger and make these forces harmless. It is to let the people have the independence they desire.

All that is why, even when the "Free" or "Fighting" Europeans were only a handful, as in 1940–41, it could be truly assumed that they represented a majority feeling in Europe. This was not then generally understood, but it was proved by the subsequent unrest and growing rebellion of Europeans under occupation. I wrote in the summer of 1941: "Before the war is over, there will be as many acts of courage and sacrifice accomplished inside France under enemy rule, as outside France under the free colors of the allies." It has come true.

It is all right to "stick to the facts," provided that all facts are taken into account. We have learned to recognize the importance of facts of opinion. We must learn, and our statesmen must learn, to recognize and give full value to facts of another kind—the facts of sentiment. They are often elusive, inarticulate and difficult to record. Yet, as facts, they may be decisive.

In 1776, George III was king of the thirteen colonies, and Colonel Washington of the Virginia militia had turned rebel. These are both facts. That a vast part of the population was in favor of Colonel Washington and his cause was a fact of opinion. That many of them were ready to lay down their lives for this cause was a fact of sentiment, as a result of which, a few years later George III was no longer king of the thirteen colonies.

Europe's interminable vigil, the terrible maturity of her children, the determination of her fighters have forged new facts—hard facts of sentiment. Any country or anyone who fails to acknowledge them, who makes his calculation without them, will make a grave mistake.

The new fact, which is of capital importance, is that men everywhere in democratic countries, having graduated as citizens, have become convinced by the force and logic of events that *a citizen is not complete if he does not possess also a sense of his international responsibility*.

THE INTERNATIONAL RESPONSIBILITIES OF MAN [1]

The essentials of democracy lie in the "rights of man." That is, of all men.

The rights of each man can serve as a basis for a demo-

[1] From *Render Unto Man*, a pamphlet printed in 1940.

cratic society only if the other men's rights are equally preserved, that is if each man professes the same respect for other men's rights that he demands for his own. That defines the democratic duties of man.

As a result, democracy is the regime which invests the individual with the maximum amount of rights and duties. Therefore with the maximum burden of personal responsibility.

Democracy is the attempt to make, as completely as is humanly possible, man responsible for his own fate.

The notion of individual responsibility is so interwoven, if not identical, with the idea of democracy, that one might well say that responsibility is to democratic life what oxygen is to our breathing: no such life is possible without it.

All undemocratic regimes, whether it is one-man dictatorship, group tyranny or mob rule, are characterized by the weakening or disappearance of that one essential: individual responsibility. And the two ways of destroying a democracy are either to suppress the rights of man, as for example in fascism, or to let him forget his duties, as in political demagogy of a type more familiar to us. In both cases, the moment a sense of full civic responsibility no longer exists, democracy virtually has gone by the board. I believe that Thomas Jefferson would subscribe to this.

It is a regime difficult to maintain. It requires full-grown minds to keep it alive. It is the most virile of regimes. The line of least effort leads to its abandonment in favor of regimes where somebody else takes care of your duties and rights—and fate—and saves you the trouble. But to a citizen, in the full sense of the term, and proud of being one, men who give up their natural rights and duties appear like eunuchs.

That democracy can work was proved materially by the fact that the most powerful, wealthiest and happiest nations in the modern world have grown to such condition under democratic regimes. That it can endure is proved by the fact that wherever a long democratic tradition has been established, people have no desire to shake it off. It has not been underlined enough that not a single democracy of old standing discarded its regime, during the recent "wave" of totalitarianism. Neither in Germany, nor Russia, nor Italy, where universal suffrage and literacy are comparatively recent, were many citizens brought up in allegiance to modern democracy. But wherever it is the product of several generations taught in civic responsibility, democracy stands. There is no exception.

* * *

Now, whether we consult the works of the founders of democracy—Locke, Montesquieu, Jefferson, Paine—or the pronouncements of our great contemporary liberals, we nowhere find that such principles and rules of behavior, which we call democratic, should stop abruptly at our national frontiers. It nowhere appears that our foreign policies, and the relations of nations with one another, should follow principles and ways which are in contradiction with the ones prevailing in our local or national life. More particularly, it was never said or implied by democratic thinkers that man was responsible for his fate except in matters international. That he had supreme duties toward the human community but not beyond his national frontier. That he was to run all his affairs except world affairs. That he should trust his own conscience, brain, courage, leadership in all matters but that in the shaping and organization of our international world, he should trust to luck. The more interdependent this world becomes, the more absurd it appears that each man should try to remain, in public affairs, half-master and half-irresponsible.

The truth that is becoming more and more apparent today, is that this world will be made either by us, or against us, and that there is no third alternative.

* * *

During the 19th Century, democracy had to conquer its existence in various places, few and far apart at first. The extent to which it succeeded is shown by the contrast, at one hundred years' distance, between the European coalition of kingdoms and empires which brought the Napoleonic wars to an end and established the Holy Alliance, and the world coalition, entirely dominated by democracies, which terminated the world war and started the League of Nations.

Yet our democratic tradition, established on generations of national experiments, is still very young as far as international life is concerned. It began in 1919. For a hundred years, even democracies had to act along undemocratic lines in their foreign relations. Secrecy, aggressiveness, oppressive deals of all sorts characterized our doings, until the time came when the masses of the people demanded in 1919 that our basic principles of civic life should be extended to international dealings. The preamble and certain articles of the League's Covenant express this resolve and emphasize its new significance. Stripped of the solemn phraseology, it says with almost naïve frankness: "From now on we must try to tell the truth . . . When a thing is forbidden it is forbidden . . . When someone makes a promise, he keeps it, or else does not deserve respect . . ." And a notable feature of the people's demand to be treated like grown-ups in their foreign relations was the abandonment of secret treaties and the solemn cancellation of all previous ones.

Yet, whereas democratic procedure was slowly penetrating international life, democracy itself was going through a crisis, extending over half a century. A crisis which has never been clearly defined by historians.

Democracy had its heroic period of self-assertion and successful experimenting. In the latter half of the 19th century, it became too successful in our Atlantic world: it came to be taken for granted. That is fatal to a creed which requires constant vigilance to maintain itself.

The colossal development of industry and material prosperity not only monopolized people's attention and efforts, it also made them indifferent to the maladies of democracy: political graft and demagogy appeared like unimportant blemishes that did not seriously threaten the health or existence of our nations. The god efficiency displaced all other creeds. America led the pace, after the war of 1861–1865, and others followed.

Well, democracy may not always afford the best conditions for material efficiency. Regimentation, collective discipline of some sort, may bring speedier results. The social foundation is less solid, but the visible achievements may be more spectacular. The material achievements of dictatorial regimes in the past few years are impressive. Fascism, nazism and communism can boast of such feats, and they do, having not much else to boast of. Democracies have a few little concrete achievements to their credit, too, but their main pride and vitality lie in the fact that people select their own lives and activities; and from a viewpoint of pure efficiency these activities often conflict.

But in the economic pursuits of our great cities our citizens, in the past few decades, laid aside their forefathers' proud claim to an individual life of their own making, and just endeavored to fit into the economic fabric wherever they could; they did whatever they were told, bought what was advertised, and indulged in an excessive amount of mass-thinking, which was not good for them as free citizens.

Evasion from civic responsibility was part of the process. Tolerance toward political corruption ("Oh, well, that's politics"), or toward the gross incapacity of elected representatives (Vachel Lindsay's exclamation: "Who elected these polecats rulers of men?") Abdication, in prosperity. Of course, people who had become irresponsible in their own city's affairs were not likely to take up world responsibilities.

The depression of 1930, almost coincident with the first aggressions against the new international order (Manchuria, 1931) played a great part in reawakening people to a sense of public duty. I was amazed to find, after 1933, both in the United States and in Europe, so many people who had never given their attention to public affairs, now deeply concerned with them.

During the coming years they may realize that if things international are drifting toward catastrophe—to their lives or to their pocketbooks—they themselves, first and last, are to blame.

There are divorces that cannot go on happily forever.

The divorce between our principles and our actions, regarding international life, was one of them.

If we are to abandon our beliefs, finding them too exacting for our weak powers of thought and action, we should have the courage of our cowardice and denounce these beliefs as conceived for a better class of men than we are.

If our ideas are rooted enough, motivated by sufficient logic and conviction within us, that only stronger ideas could displace them, and if the dictators have failed to supply these stronger ideas—then let us do what our beliefs command. But walking on the divergent paths of constructive thinking and destructive behavior, cannot last much longer. Either our conduct will result in the kind of world that our thought abhors and despises, or our thinking will put an end to such conduct.

The time has come for every individual to make up his mind as to what category he belongs to: an obedient subject, a passive unit in the adventure of collective life, or a full citizen.

Where man accepts his individual responsibilities in full, he soon discovers that they include leadership in world affairs,—a share in it at least. There is no escape from this gradual rise of our men and women to world responsibility; or else it would mean that the world is to take shape under the leadership of others.

THE AMERICAN ANGLE

> *"If it were given to me to look into the depth of a man's heart and I did not find good will at the bottom, I should say without any hesitation, you are not an American."*
>
> GEORGE SANTAYANA

AMERICA IN THE DISTANCE (1920–1941)

THE POSITION OF AMERICA IN REGARD TO THE INEVITABLE developments in Europe, to-day and in the future, is an outcome of recent American history.

The U.S. grew from a condition of almost total ignorance and irresponsibility concerning world affairs, in 1920, to a state of well-documented concern. Twenty-five years ago, not more than 1% of the American people had any ideas on international affairs. When the second world war broke out in 1939, probably 15% took an active interest and felt a national concern.

This was a result of the remarkable work accomplished by the best newspapers, associations, colleges and individuals, to educate at least part of the public towards its inevitable responsibilities.

I remember a good-humored cartoon in an American pro-League paper in 1920. A crowd of leisurely looking bathers, labeled with the names of various countries, were wading in a shallow pool, called the League of Nations. In the middle of the pool, a stout John Bull with water up to his ankles shouted to Uncle Sam, who stood terrified on the shore dressed in several life-belts, roped to an anchor and tied to a strong tree: "Come on, Sam! If it were dangerous, would I be in it?"

During the hopeful years, news and comments about European affairs were scarce in the American press and magazines; news and comments about the League were practically taboo. It was not until 1927 that normal contact was re-established, when the United States took part, with all other nations, in the Economic Conference held at Geneva.

The following year saw the presentation of the Kellogg-Briand Pact for the renunciation of war. It is a bitter irony that such a step, the first bold one taken by the United States, should have preceded by one year only the crisis in Wall Street. America had but one brief year to watch the League work successfully.

How did the trouble begin?

First, the death of Stresemann. And shortly after, the effects in Europe of the Wall Street crash of November 1929, and the economic depression that followed. Germany, heavily industrialized, all her existing and borrowed wealth invested in modern industrial equipment, and everything staked on a successful economic expansion, was hit first and hardest. Unemployment, the shrinking of all her markets, coupled with political inexperience in the ways of democracy, produced such sufferings and disappointments throughout 1930 that the people lost confidence in their own capacity to run their affairs, and the

Nazis with their simplified slogans and easy remedies had their chance. Their first victory, in September 1930, was like the sudden growth of an infection on a healing sore. Mr. Hitler at once engaged in his lusty practice of tearing off the bandages on all of Germany's old wounds exclaiming: "Look how you bleed!"

Germany was an easy prey to a regime and to the ideas which she had resisted and rejected during the first years of her democratic existence.

The next step towards the disintegration of our peace system was Japan's aggression against China on September 18, 1931.

The two most important neighbors of Japan, namely Russia and the United States, were not members of the League. The Council had no leadership because Briand, who presided, was in the last months of his life and his vitality was gone. Stresemann was dead. Sir John Simon did not take the lead. General Dawes, sent as an observer, did not come near the Council meetings. The Japanese saw what a dispersed, inefficient team they had in front of them. And they made a goal, that is, they stayed in Manchuria.

In the following year, Mr. Stimson came to Geneva and tried to induce the other powers to some more active policy of resistance, but it was too late.

In 1933, both Japan and Germany announced their withdrawal from the League, and Germany completely sabotaged the Disarmament Conference after a stage had been reached which gave promise of early success. The Nazis and the Japanese did not want the conference to succeed, because it would have made their armament programs much more difficult to achieve. They wanted to catch the Western nations in a peaceful, sleepy mood, in a mood to restrict their military expenditures and trust to luck; Germany and Japan could then steal two or three years advantage in rearmament. They succeeded.

The plan was spoiled slightly by the Italian aggression of 1935 against Ethiopia. It awakened a part of British and French opinion to the immediate danger to their colonies, their sea communications, and to the inadequacy of their defenses. It started England and France on ideas of rearmament, somewhat earlier than Germany wished.

In the meantime, the forces of peace forged ahead for several years, gaining support, in a race which was finally lost, after aggression had several times been allowed to proceed unchecked.

America, in these days, disapproved of Europe's "fears." What did Europe fear? In America the depression was a far more important experience than a world war; in Europe the war, a personal everpresent memory, remained the principal fear of the people.

Part of it was legitimate fear, based on dangers which existed. We were accused of thinking too much in terms of danger. Perhaps if Mexico had 200 million inhabitants, and her armies had advanced as far as Washington, D. C., two or three times during the last century, Americans would have felt more nervous about such dangers. The United States had had as many wars as any European nation during this century, but each time it went to war of its own free will and each time it was victorious. Before December 1941, never had war been imposed on it, as it was, say, on Belgium in 1914 and again in 1940.

The story of the following years is a story of how men shut their eyes to the obvious. The United States enjoyed the privilege of blissful aloofness; but all the time, the kind of world wherein America could grow more and more prosperous was deteriorating, and materials were being assembled for the kind of world where there would be no place for democratic America.

The Hoover moratorium of 1931 and the American participation in the Disarmament Conference of 1932 were steps to protect American interests and to further American policy rather than full-fledged acts of world collaboration. More significant was American membership in the International Labor Organization, but participation in the Permanent Court of International Justice at the Hague was never obtained, due to the rule in the American Senate by which a minority of one third can impose its will on a majority of two thirds.

The gravest misunderstanding between American public opinion and opinion in most countries which were members of the League consisted, on the part of Americans, in believing that other nations were over anxious to secure a commitment by the United States to lend their armed forces to any international action against an eventual violator of the Covenant or of the Paris Pact. On the other hand Europeans believed that Americans were unwilling to do anything in case peace should be violated. Implicit encouragement was given to any prospective violator who otherwise might fear American opposition.

As a matter of fact, American armed intervention was far from being the most efficient, immediate or desirable form of help for a victim of an aggression.

There might have been a number of steps, "short of war," by which the American nation might have given powerful help to the international endeavor to enforce peace.

In 1935, American opinion had not really crystallized about the League. There were a few irreconcilables, a few enthusiasts, and of course the masses to whom the question had not been put in any pressing terms since 1920.

Partisans of American participation in the League were professors, writers, lawyers, ministers, women's groups and the best newspapers. Contrary to the experience in Europe, neither ex-service men nor labor showed much interest. The prospect of a majority favorable to American membership was still remote. Yet a poll in the Republican state of Massachusetts, of 116 towns and villages and covering about one third of the State's population, showed a majority of 62% in favor of American membership in the League.

Most members of the Roosevelt Cabinet were favorable to the League. So were many prominent Republicans— Henry Stimson, President Nicholas Murray Butler, Frank Knox, Frank Coudert, etc. There remained the "irreconcilables," Borah and Johnson, who with the help of the Hearst press, *The Nation* and the *New Republic*, had defeated Wilson in 1920.[1]

In early 1935, a stampede in the American Senate, under the joint influences of Father Coughlin, Senator Huey

[1] Reactionaries and "progressives" had opposite motives in that fight, but to us the result was the same: Wilson's defeat and the ensuing setback. As world citizens, we are not interested in the "liberal" motives of part of the opposition.

Long and Mr. Hearst, defeated the proposal for participation in the World Court.[1]

In the meantime, as a modern complement to politics, the debunking of history made remarkable progress.

The Senate inquiry about private traffic in arms led the amateur historians of the investigating committee presided over by Senator Nye to an over-simplified but star-

[1] Asked by the *New York Times* to state my views on this subject, I answered:

"That a measure was defeated because fifty-two senators had voted in favor of it, and thirty-six against, will be very difficult to explain to people throughout the world. . . . Here is a splendid opportunity for misunderstanding.

"I hear statements to the effect that the American people were 'overwhelmingly' against world cooperation. At the same time, every poll, every popular consultation or college vote, every contact I have had personally, show that Americans wish to help in organizing and maintaining world peace. In a proportion probably stronger than the senatorial sixty per cent majority in favor of the World Court, church groups, Labor groups, Leagues of Women Voters, granges, bar associations, newspapers, have gone on record as favoring various forms of world association, provided that it would not involve America against her will in an action that her people would not support. Then, as the saying goes, 'What is wrong in the picture?'

"What puzzles me, in my desire to respect and understand, and eventually to interpret and explain to my compatriots the position of America, is the question: 'What *is* the real position of America?'

"Will it be that of the President plus the elite of the country, plus the majority of the people, plus sixty per cent of the Senate? No! They were defeated. They don't represent America.

"Shall it be, then, the minority? But my people know that America is a democracy, and if I give them a minority opinion as the national opinion, they won't believe me.

"They will be further puzzled when they hear that solid opposition to the World Court came from representatives of supposedly liberal voters, as in the Northwest. In the rest of the world, Court and League supporters are to be found among the liberal and radical masses and opposition comes from the militaristic and reactionary forces.

"As a conclusion, I have only one suggestion to make, but I make it quite seriously. It is this. Now that the American minority has successfully made known to the world its position, for the sake of clarity, let the American majority also find some way of expressing its will."

tling interpretation of American intervention in 1917: that Woodrow Wilson obeyed the orders of bankers, and bankers were controlled by the merchants of death. That explained everything.

In 1936, Neutrality legislation was enacted. A brief survey of American opinion showed three dominant currents:

I. Industrial, farming and exporting interests insisted on the traditional freedom of the seas and open foreign markets, and resented too rigorous curtailment of their profits.

II. Isolationism, which catered to the first instinctive reaction of the masses against foreign trouble. It was allied to a genuine but summary form of pacifism which consisted in ignoring war, "having nothing to do with it," and therefore not cooperative.

III. Thinking groups, which tended to treat war not as an inevitable calamity, but as a human evil which could be fought and cured, and aggression as something to be prevented.

Supporters of this constructive tendency had to fight on two fronts: against the brutal selfishness of those who might sabotage peace for immediate profit, and the demagogic or naïve insistence on an unconditional isolation, which would ruin America and would not prevent war.

The neutrality legislation came as a compromise.

The Executive was not satisfied; the Senate was not satisfied; the peace groups were not satisfied; the isolationists were not satisfied and the people who tried to build up a system of international cooperation were not satisfied. Moreover, each time the legislation had to be applied it had also to be amended. (It began with the amendment concerning the 21 American Republics: in their case the law would not be applied because the American people were against letting them be attacked and controlled by foreign powers.)

At the Brussels conference of November 1937, which I attended, the Chinese delegation presented a brief memorandum discreetly entitled, "Some data showing the possibilities of taking certain economic and financial measures to stop Japanese aggression in China."

In an objective form, and with simple figures, it showed to what extent an aggressor may depend on the great nations who dispose of the world's raw materials.

In time of peace, Japan imported 90% of its oil, 56% of its iron, and so all along the list of essentials.

Most of these imports came from the three or four countries who wished most ardently that hostilities in China should come to a close.

The peaceful powers had adopted on October 6th, with the immediate approval of the United States, a resolution which recommended that they abstain from anything tending to weaken China in her legitimate resistance. At the same time, they kept supplying Japan with all the means of intensifying her action. When we think of Japan's admitted objectives, we wonder if in the name of the sacrosanct dogma of immediate profit, all sense of elementary safety had not been lost.

The Chinese memorandum showed that in 1936 the British Empire bought 26% of Japanese exports, the United States 24%, China 6%, the Dutch Indies 5%, France and her possessions 1.75%.

The memorandum concluded by calling attention to what an embargo would mean to the big industrial and commercial interests in Japan, which already showed little enthusiasm for war. And boycott would have been fatal to the Japanese gold reserve.

These were relevant facts. Some statesmen spoke of "quarantine" applied to aggressors. By putting two and two together, perhaps we might have gotten somewhere.

In 1938, there were in America very strong feelings in favor of four different systems, each of them containing some of the American tradition:

1. Absolute isolation, even at the risk of grave losses in money and prestige.
2. A vigorous policy in support of American interests, but in the form of independent action, without any joint commitment with other nations. The old Theodore Roosevelt big stick.
3. A prudent collaboration with other nations, mostly on lines of economic and social realizations, with a maximum of freedom of decision in things political, with general aims and principles similar to those of other "peace-loving" nations. That was Mr. Hull's policy.
4. Accepted solidarity with democratic nations in order to form a peace front that would be more powerful than any combination of aggressors. In other terms, resurrection of an efficient League of Nations, in which the United States would take its full share. That policy was desired by a comparatively small elite, including leaders who were Woodrow Wilson's disciples.

These various "parties" had evolved in various ways, during the last twenty years. On the whole, the partisans of isolation (passive or active) had constantly been losing ground. Partisans of close international solidarity had not gained much. It is the partisans of cautious and progressive collaboration who were the winners.

Americans were divided on the efficiency and opportunity of methods to be followed, not on the aims, which were peace and the protection of American economic interests. According to their degree of information, and confidence in the other democratic countries (there was no confidence whatever in totalitarian States) Americans were more, or less, prepared to consent to world collaboration.

The party of wholesale isolation had no eminent champion of its theory, but was in accord with the instincts and habits of uninformed masses flattered by demagogic politicians and newspapers. The party of "every nation to itself" had strong roots in the traditions of a powerful country with no dangerous neighbors. Yet it had lost ground, because such policy was in accord with neither the pacific aspirations of the people, nor the realities of the world.

President Roosevelt, on repeated occasions, expressed America's preferences and dislikes toward the various systems that ruled the nations of the world. To the democratic nations, his words gave encouragement and support, even though they were only words. That was the only contribution America could give in her mood at that time.[1]

[1] In France, his voice was heard. On the day of his Buenos Aires speech, the French government, on my suggestion, ordered that a full translation should be broadcast on the State radio system "so that every village could have knowledge of it." Five days later, the best French political weekly, *l'Europe Nouvelle*, published a 12,000 word supplement, which I had compiled, quoting the most significant passages of Mr. Roosevelt's and Mr. Hull's principal speeches on foreign affairs between March 1933 and December 1936.

Between 1940 and 1944, it can be assumed that the proportion of the American public which understands world affairs beyond the headlines, and takes a constructive stand about them, has grown from 15% to approximately 50%. The United States has reached to-day the degree of world consciousness which England had attained between 1920 and 1925. An indication to this effect is that the commitments for which the U.S. people were ready in late 1944 correspond about exactly to those which the British became ready to accept twenty years ago. Locarno, yes, but not the Geneva protocol.

The process of American awakening to world facts will appear relatively speedy to historians of the future; 25 years is a short period. But to those of us who lived through that period and had a clear and burning vision of what American leadership could have accomplished, this evolution appeared painfully, sometimes unbearably slow.

When the German invasion rolled over Western Europe in the Spring of 1940, the confusion in people's minds was a result either of previous misinformation or of bad habits of thought. Otherwise the situation was clear enough: a European war was becoming a world war, because in the long run the world could not and would not accept a German victory. But the world, especially the U.S., did not know exactly what it could or could not accept, because it had never thought about it. Dunkirk and the French armistice compelled them to think.

The efforts of many people to evade this thinking was pathetic and almost grandiose. It was as if they had such a poor opinion of their own brains that any sacrifice, even of life itself, would have been better than working out the process of logic and reason.

AMERICAN LEADERSHIP, PRESENT OR ABSENT

To those of us who in 1940 were passionately engaged in the task of awakening the American public to the facts of the world crisis, it appeared evident that the world could not escape some form of organization. It would be accomplished by us, or against us, and there was no third choice.

In the case of an Allied victory, the hope for a decent future was in some efficient Anglo-American leadership. It would be welcome to all peace-loving nations, as it would respect their independence and help to coordinate the normal economic activities of all countries.

In the case of a Nazi victory, hundreds of millions of people would live under foreign rule, in a state of sullen or open rebellion. Where would be the leadership for that rebellion?

America, whether she knew it or not, would have been the last headquarters of liberty.

Instead of being driven reluctantly to such a position of leadership, why didn't the American people accept it and take hold of it cheerfully and see it through in the American way?

That they should have had only a mild interest in the re-drafting of European boundaries could be easily understood. But there was more at stake: the shaping of a new world, if it was to escape the Nazi-made "new order."

Once this opportunity was made clear, the American task would not seem like an undesirable burden, but the most inspiring call, ever to be heard and answered by a nation.

Had the revolution for man's personal rights, initiated

and carried on with America's inspiration and example, spent itself? Was the human race drifting back along counter-revolutionary lines towards a restoration of the old hierarchy of masters, subjects and slaves? Or did the present conflict, beyond denominations and abstractions, bring a revival of man's undying capacity to struggle for the control of his own fate?

The United States alone in the world had enjoyed a nearly complete freedom of decision in its foreign policies. Every one of its wars had been undertaken because the nation so elected. Which led Americans to believe that nations fought wars only when they wanted to, and that if anybody was engaged in war it must be that he liked it. But that happy epoch of American isolation and liberty of choice was over. America was in this world and of this world, a world in danger of promptly becoming the kind of place where Americans would not care to live.

With the outside world under totalitarian rule, the idea of America as an independent paradise, giving a fine example of peace, good government and happiness to the rest of the nations, was utopian, were it only because dictators could not afford to allow such a dangerous example to exist before the eyes of their conquered subjects, or even their own people. Moreover, an all-powerful alliance of dictators that would respect and leave intact American wealth, living space and natural resources would not resemble the kind of world empire that we saw emerging from the German victories in the first phase of this war.

America had to realize that, if England did not destroy Hitler, liberty would be blown out here and would have nowhere on earth to go.

There would have been no American refugees.

A world under Anglo-American leadership? Many of us accepted the choice and said *yes* to such a world. In 1940, the English and the American empires seemed the only two powers who could:

1. Group the other people with their consent into a world organization acceptable to all.
2. Lead in the efficient enforcement of peace.

All they had to do was to extend to the whole planet the rules that had proved successful in the building up of their own commonwealths.

A huge task was ahead, but not insuperable if men did not shrink from all effort, saying either: "This was tried before, yet look at what happened," or else: "It was never tried before, this is no time for experimenting."

A world republic, that is, a federation of free countries inhabited by free people, was an enterprise which called for the collaboration of all, and the leadership of the best. The material for it already existed. Mankind had still a chance to save itself.

If this was not enough to fire the imagination and challenge creative powers, then what would?

Four years ago, we were a few who assumed that the American people would rapidly see the world picture, and their own task, in such a light.

Well, it did not happen exactly that way.

The good people who joined William Allen White's Committee to Defend America by Aiding the Allies devoted considerable efforts to proving what should have been obvious from the start; that if America wished Hitler to be defeated, something ought to be done about it. Venturing beyond that prudent proposition was forbidden, in the interest of the campaign. Aiding England "short of war" was the slogan, which fell short of the need through fear of antagonizing the people with the whole truth. Sugar-coating is such an accepted part of promotion, that even promoting national safety had to keep to the approved method. We were constantly reminded of what *not* to tell, from among the facts of life, because "the American public would not like to hear it," or "was not ready for it," or "had never heard of it."

A very few people were impatient with this infantile approach. Some of them created the so-called "Westport group," which started calling a spade a spade, in 1941, and demonstrated the need for immediate action. They could not go very far, in spite of their talent, courage and sincerity.

The obstacle was not so much with the pro-fascists or isolationists. It was with the vast, shapeless, boneless but innumerable majority that did not wish to be disturbed in its "way of life." As to most political leaders, they had adopted the well-known attitude of sitting on the fence with both ears to the ground, which is not such a difficult trick if the ears are long enough.

Even after America had been attacked and had embarked on her formidable industrial war effort, the same allergy to ideas prevailed within large groups. As late as 1943, one met with the statement that all thinking was "premature" and only arms and ammunition were needed. In nine cases out of ten this came from people who were *not* engaged in the making of arms and ammunition. They had simply found a convenient justification for their allergy.

In the meantime, one category of Americans—the press and radio foreign correspondents—was performing a magnificent job. I am not exaggerating when I say that theirs was the major American contribution to the saving of our civilization.

This was not the result of a special selection. They were good ordinary Americans who lived in close touch with world realities. They were able to demonstrate what remarkable powers of common sense, human understanding and accuracy of vision, not to mention courage, exist in the average American and find expression once he is taken out of his cellophane wrapping.

Their accounts were true, direct, and prophetic. The American public read the stories but discounted the prophecies, since these men were supposedly "influenced by foreign atmosphere" and out of touch with the American reality. But examine today the writings and the speeches of Edmund Taylor, Leland Stowe, Jay Allen, Anne O'Hare McCormick, Edgar Mowrer, Raymond Swing, William Shirer, Ed Murrow, John Gunther, Herbert Matthews, Quentin Reynolds, Eric Sevareid, C. L. Sulzberger, Ernie Pyle and numerous others, and try to find a body of statesmen in any country who have made so few mistakes and pursued the truth with more ardor and talent. They did more than serve the public. They proved to the world what American brains can accomplish, once they are made use of.

In December 1941, war came to America. A definite way to win the war was dictated by circumstances, geographical position and industrial capacity for production. The U.S. had a formidable industrial potential, out of reach of the enemy. It had a large population, industrially minded, and untrained in actual military activities. For the common good, America increased her production to a maximum. Thus the "arsenal of democracy" intensified its own peacetime aspect.

So the U.S. had the unique experience of playing a major part in the war *without* changing fundamentally its ways of life. It rushed into this material effort that provided more and better paid jobs for more people. Physical activity, of a type already familiar, intensified in the service of a righteous aim, what could be easier to accept? In the midst of world chaos and revolution, America was *hyper-normal*, and Americans did not have to think much about the meaning of their cause, since they had been attacked. The simplest slogans would do. "Back 'em up"; "Back the attack"; "Let 'em have it." That was enough.

So when the test came of showing understanding of what the war was all about, results were far from satisfactory. We do not mean to insist on the Habsburg, Darlan, Giraud, Badoglio episodes which only reflect the usual innocence and misinformation of foreign offices in matters of foreign popular feeling. America did not do any worse than England and France did during World War I in regard to Russia, or in 1912 in regard to the Balkans, or all of our governments in 1936 in regard to Spain.

But leaving aside governments, sentiment in world affairs cannot spring at a moment's notice from mere intuition. The truth is that as late as the two great political conventions of 1944, American public sentiment was reluctant to even tackle such affairs, let alone place them at the top of the list of vital preoccupations.

With unfailing instinct the delegates of both parties, for

fear of losing votes, eliminated the candidates who had drawn attention to themselves for their major interest in world affairs, even though those men were of a high ethical and intellectual caliber.

A wide-awake and vigorous support for American leadership in foreign affairs cannot be expected from labor, farmers, businessmen, the American Legion, nor the manufacturers. Where, then, can it come from?

Mr. Cordell Hull, in a formal statement to the press on August 17, 1944, said with his usual frankness that "there is not as yet in the United States a public opinion by any means sufficiently informed or alert enough to support any practical peace organization." No matter how much progress the reading public has made in twenty years, no matter how clear the international thinking of a few may be at the present time, the truth remains that as far as active and conscious world *leadership* is concerned, America as a whole has not entirely caught up with the times.

As to the great American writers such as Waldo Frank or Lewis Mumford, who rank among the real prophets of our time, it is a fact that the public hardly knows their names.

POSITION OF THE U.S. TO-DAY

My faith remains unbroken in American potential leadership in a not too distant future. My illusion in 1940 was to believe that the time had come.

There is no discredit in being the most conservative country in the world. Some country has to be.

Americans, like the Swiss, have excellent reasons to be

conservative. They have good things to conserve, such as principles, social and political, which once were new and daring. But that was 150 years ago. Just as the Pullman car because of its novelty and comfort was an object of admiration for the world in 1875. It is no longer.

Americans who are still under the impression that their country is at the vanguard of political and social thought should be reminded that England and France have had Labor or Socialist prime ministers; that in the French parliament at the last elections (1936) there were more than 25% socialists and 11% communists; that Sweden, a conservative country, has 50% social-democrats; and that Mr. Wallace, who in America is classified a radical, would be considered a middle-of-the-road statesman everywhere else, even in Switzerland.

In America, ever since the Revolution, very little has happened to interfere with the American way—social, political, ethical or spiritual. As the American experiment was eminently successful, almost nobody questions the Constitution. Why should it be questioned?[1] Yet how many countries in the world have lived on the same constitution for 150 years and are still pleased with it?

American history in the 20th century was marked by a series of threatened crises. Twice in the last fifteen years catastrophes passed closely by. In March 1933, after the closing of the banks, the looting of grocery stores by orderly citizens was just beginning to endanger American society; and in 1941 Hitler wasted his forces against Rus-

[1] A friend of mine made this remark: "Only three amendments to the Constitution have amounted to a real change: one said that Negroes should enjoy equal rights, and they still don't; one said that people shouldn't drink, and they still do; one said that women should have power, and they always had."

sia, while Japan drove south, instead of joining with Germany to gang up against the American continent.

As a result of this last piece of luck, America had enough time for her splendid effort of production and organization. The result is victory. But the American people will never realize what almost happened to them. And this makes them fundamentally different from the nations to whom everything happened. I do not mean inferior or superior, merely different.

U.S. WORLD PLANS

American world plans, as they appear to-day, either sponsored by the President or the State Department, or suggested by responsible groups of first-class experts, or presented in the individual writings of Mr. Walter Lippmann, Mr. Sumner Welles, or others, are all a product of constructive thinking combined with that special brand of intellectual pragmatism, which characterizes America.

These men know all there is to know about world affairs. But they want to be useful, not just brilliant. They calculate how much of their independent thinking can be dealt out to the public, so that the public will absorb it and support a good foreign policy. They are right because an American foreign policy must have public support, or collapse. As a result, their plans include only such items as are compatible with the present mood of the people and Congress.

The trouble is that the mood will change, and therefore the policy and the aims will vary with the platforms of the Republican and Democratic parties. By now, Europe knows that. Therefore, Europe is likely to watch the foundation of an American foreign policy with extreme interest and sympathy, but unlike 1919 when America was counted on as the keystone of the new international order, Europe now will count primarily on herself.

The conference at Dumbarton Oaks illustrated the fact that America was at the same time deeply desirous of promoting world peace, and only at the early stage of realizing what it requires. The tentative proposals set forth by the U.S., Russia, England and China bore a very close resemblance to the League Covenant of 1919: in many respects identical, but with some general principles omitted and some definite commitments carefully evaded. This is not the place for a detailed analysis of the scheme. Let us recall that of the four great powers represented, the U.S. never joined the League, Russia joined it after 14 years and was expelled five years later, and China received little protection from her membership. England was the only power present at Dumbarton Oaks, whose policy had been to consistently support and make use of the League. No wonder if the League as such was not referred to. But the situation will be a very different one when some 50 or 60 "peace-loving countries" participate in the new world organization. Practically all of them have been loyal members of the League, and feel no need of camouflaging their old allegiance under a new façade and new names. They will recognize and state the fact that we are back in 1919 confronted with the same problem of world organization, but with the essential difference that America and Russia are with us from the start. If things go well and the "new" organization gets under way, we shall be confronted with the situation which prevailed in 1924, when medium-sized and small nations grouped around France complained that the Covenant was not binding and specific enough, and supported the Geneva Protocol which would have put teeth and efficiency into it. At that same time, England and her dominions regarded the Covenant as rather too binding, and refused to commit themselves any further.

England has evolved since. She does not believe any more that her security rests "on the Channel," or "on the Rhine." Arthur Henderson in 1934 said that it rested on the Covenant. Therefore, a close security system on the lines of the Geneva protocol is likely to reappear on a regional basis, because England and the Liberated Nations of Europe are ready for it.

This leads to the acceptance of *several* security circles, defined precisely by that readiness of various nations to pay a more or less high insurance premium, in the form of mutual limitations of sovereignty. And this is as it should be, since a single security system for all would prove either too binding for America, or else neither specific nor efficient enough for Europe.

THE U.S. AND THE NEW EUROPE

Let us now attempt to examine the new European prospects from a strictly American angle.

These prospects will naturally provoke various reactions: favorable, skeptical or panicky. Leaving aside the millions who don't care and don't wish to know, there are other millions who could be led easily to unreasoned fear toward the new and unexpected.

Just as Hearst, Borah, and Oswald Garrison Villard used to fan the instinctive distrust and hostility toward foreign problems and a warring Europe, similar influences will excite the same hostility toward a united Europe. Those same people who were slow to wake up to the peril of a Hitlerian Europe, may be quick to fear the peril of a reconciled and strong Europe.

In fact, the only perils which might arise for America would result from that very fear. Europe has no motive and no desire to adopt an unfriendly attitude toward the New World; on the contrary. But if the New World should antagonize Europe, it would result fatally in her looking for other friends. She would find them in the East, and if the whole process resulted in a banding together of Europe, China and India (although America would have been Europe's first choice) the world would be threatened with another secession, fraught with dangers which are now avoidable.

Europe, as we see it crystallizing, leans equally on England and on Russia for its balance. This is a favorable condition to prevent the undesirable hegemony of any single power. But if the Anglo-Saxon powers were ill-inspired enough to try for a commercial or political hegemony over Europe, the result can be predicted with certainty: Europe, seeking support against encroachments, would lean toward Russia. Similarly, Europe would veer closer to England and America if Russian imperialism showed its hand too indiscreetly.

Chaos in Europe would be disastrous for American interests, for reasons which are clear enough. It would mean sooner or later a relapse into situations calling for American armed intervention. On the other hand, any machiavelian policy of "divide et impera" in Europe, on the part of the U.S., could only lead to more conflicts from which America could not remain aloof. Nor is there any reason why American diplomacy would succeed at a game where the Germans failed. The true American way, of peace, equality and prosperity for all, is infinitely sounder and more likely to succeed. And it should be obvious that American industry has everything to gain by the opening of new markets in Europe and the rapid rise of European buying power.

The "un-American" attitude would be to jeopardize or retard this normal development, through fear of change.

AMERICA WILL BE PROMISES

During these last twenty years, I tried more than once to imagine what Thomas Jefferson would have said, and would have done, had he been faced with our contemporary problems.

I believe that he would have stood for the League of Nations.

I believe that he would have dealt fearlessly with the world problem as a whole, recognizing the unity of mankind and the interdependence of national groups. Confident as he was in the people's ultimate ability to take care of their own fate, he would have trusted the democratic way of life to outlive its enemies. With the formidable optimism of our forefathers, an optimism that was justified and vindicated more often than it was thwarted and deceived, he would have thrown the tremendous weight, both material and spiritual, of this Republic into the scales.

May I say that there have been moments when people of the outside world had more faith in the United States and its mission, than Americans seemed to profess themselves? In 1920, the slogan was: "Let us mind our own backyard." Yet at that time millions of men and women were placing their hope in American leadership. During these twenty years, only the best among Americans had kept a vivid sense of what American leadership had meant and could mean. But we French never ceased to know it. We would not, and we could not forget America.

Events, in spite of political slogans, made you ever present among us, for better or for worse.

American example transformed our old-fashioned industrial methods into modern ones.

America sent two million men to end war in Europe and to free fifty million people from foreign rule.

America took the lead in creating, for the first time in history, a Society of Nations in order to enforce peace and to settle international disputes by peaceful procedure.

America decided not to be a member of that Society of Nations.

America, however, took again the lead in renouncing the sovereign right to resort to war as an instrument of national policy. Sixty nations signed with you that renunciation and fifty-seven of them lived up to their pledge.

The American financial crisis of 1929 came as a destructive shock to the world's economic life, shattered Germany's recovery, and contributed to the rise of Nazi power —a direct result of economic desperation.

An American President, in 1931 and 1932, managed that the German reparations should be wiped out, so that Germany could put her resources to peaceful enterprise and forget about war. You know the result.

The American Congress put an embargo on all war supplies to belligerents.

American public opinion lifted that embargo in October, 1931.

America decided to become the arsenal of democracy and of resistance to aggression.

Americans landed in North Africa, in Sicily and in France . . .

In each case, millions of lives in the rest of the world were affected, for better or worse, by your decisions. Millions of people have been saved or doomed, fired to great hopes or thrown into ruin and despair, as a direct result of what happened in the supposedly isolated United States. It seems to me that Thomas Jefferson would have taken a prominent interest in all this. He had vision, and to him more than to anyone else, "America was promises."

We, Europeans, insist that it still is.

NEW CHARTS

MEN AGAINST MAN

THE DANGER, IN A CHANGING WORLD, IS TO CLING TO WHAT is dying, and at the same time be paralyzed by fear of its inevitable death.

This world is covered with ashes, not only of exploded towns. It is strewn with the dead or dying remnants of obsolete habits and creeds. This is where the great god Shiva steps in.

Shiva is the god of necessary destruction, therefore of welcome purification. His fire consumes the dead leaves and the corpses, his floods wash away the ruins, the dead fears and the dead loves. He purifies and prepares the naked souls of men for new revelations. He is the god who throws away the heavy clothing and meaningless attributes to make possible the new laughter, the dance and the forgetting of past tortures. He achieves the confused and unfinished work of men. He is the one who kills what is dead. We are in great need of him.

He is welcomed only by the strong. Others are afraid of remaining without anything at all, should they be deprived of their dead possessions. The strong do not cling to dead possessions.

False realism and false efficiency were the dangerous drugs. They caused men to work against man. They lured men into tasks and enterprises which went against the grain of man. Contemporary civilization, having a nice bird in its hand, let it go in order to catch one million birds in the bush. Only there was no bush.

False hopes have deceived men and nations: hopes of shortcuts to power, to wealth, to domination. The patient human ways were abandoned for the sake of bigger and quicker results. Look at the results.

For the strong, there is no wishful whimpering about lost paradises or present-day hell. There is the look ahead —across and beyond the present and the near future, to a fate which can still be of our making.

This is what the real believers in democracy meant by giving man a maximum of opportunity. The men of Europe, once they have recaptured their lost chance of mastering their own fate, will not easily drop it again.

There was a time when we thought that efficiency required first the enlistment of large numbers, the extension of a "movement" until it included groups of all descriptions, making an imposing total. Well, each group added a fetter to the original, vigorous and genuine program of the founders. Compromise, then more compromise, for the sake of a large membership. Growing irresponsibility on the part of the individuals. In the end a shapeless, spineless, purposeless but enormous mass. Unwieldy, capable only of vague and ineffectual reactions. It is because we saw multiple examples of the impotence of such massive bodies that I urge a return to man, a revival of the personal activities and responsibilities of men and women who know where they want to go.

It is only after citizens have thought out, selected, and resolved upon their course of action, that they should look around for allies, for fellow citizens who have arrived at the same choice and resolution. Then their alliance will be worth something. I know that this is not the totalitarian way. It is the opposite of the totalitarian method of assembling terrified people and imposing upon them some common creed that will restore their sense of being alive.

Remember the oath that the mountaineers from the Spanish and French Pyrenees used to pronounce in the presence of their king:

"We, each of whom is worth as much as you are, and who together are more powerful than you are, we offer you allegiance if you respect our freedom and our rights. And if not, no."

BEYOND DEMOCRACY

In the ten resisting countries of Europe, the resistance produced a sort of superdemocracy, a companionship by mutual election, which may well be a preview of regimes to come. It came about as a result of heroic circumstances, which were a test of men and leaders.

In the Underground, not words and promises, but acts and tenacious constancy of purpose determined the choice of leaders. Their followers were volunteers. So there was brought about the authentic human relations that democracy is supposed to create.

As long as men are capable of such relations, why could they not be produced by education and by civic consciousness, instead of by the necessities of war? Can't instinct plus education make people capable of sacrifice? Education has produced among civilians a readiness to respond to the call of arms and at a moment's notice to give their lives, against a foreign enemy. It is possible, now that democracy has been both chastised and vindicated by what has happened during these four years, that it will produce a veritable aristocracy, as a result of *intelligent election*, and that the people, instead of returning to the low standards of half-demagogy will insist on maintaining the high standards which determined their choice when the Gestapo was watching them. In fact, this is precisely the tendency which is being manifested in the countries already liberated. Leaders seem to be selected according to their record as patriots and as men. Whether this will be permanent or not, nobody can tell at this time.

VOCATION AND FREEDOM

There is a revolution in the making within men which will assign a new meaning to their work, in complete opposition to the meaning implied by totalitarianism.

If this ever takes the form of a slogan, it will be something like "the job is for the man, not the man for the job"; or in other words "Here is the man; what shape should a job take, to fit him?" In contrast to the prevailing attitude, since the industrial revolution, taken by capitalists and communists alike: "Here is the job; let a man adjust himself to it."

This book is not the place for a discussion of such an idea. But let us remember that the American depression following 1929 brought a rediscovery of their vocations to many young Americans. Because the fallacy of getting-rich-quick without effort through the approved methods had been exploded, there was a freer choice of activity. In the same way Europeans who, having lost everything, have recovered their freedom, know what it is worth and will cling to it more ardently than before. They will demand not only political freedom, but also freedom to choose an occupation and to shape it according to their capacities, desires, and requirements. I saw this happening to my younger countrymen before this war. They were beginning to make for themselves existences and occupations often less profitable, but more in harmony with the person they wanted to be. It was still possible, in Europe, to make a job fit the person. I believe that this will be intensified, contrary to the tendencies of one or two generations ago, which were toward standardization. Standardization is *more than ever* in order, as applied to the inanimate. As applied to man, its results are more and more revolting, and we seem to realize it.[1]

If this should be true, then the nightmare of man enslaved by his machines will be dispelled. Totalitarianism, that supermachine, carried the notion of quantitative efficiency to its utmost and absurd consequences. So it forced man to wake up and rebel.

Civilization, then, can resume its normal growth—until something worse happens to it.

RENDER UNTO MAN

For nearly two hundred years, we have been accustomed to speak in terms of "mankind." Philosophers of the 18th century, statesmen of the 19th, and politicians in the 20th, have taken mankind as the object of their studies,

[1] This appears in a striking form in such films as René Clair's "A nous la liberté" and Chaplin's "Modern Times," which are extremely important documents on the *reaction* against a previous trend.

and their tactics. Politicians came to adopt easy generalities designed to deal with the abstract average man, leaving the individual man to the poet and the novelist. In politics, he was the forgotten cell in a glorified body. It became one of the tricks of demagogy to enlist mass support on the fictitious assumption that the individual happiness of each supporter would result, as a matter of course, from the political success of the party, of the class, or of the nation. And so, "men went on contributing their personal misery to collective prosperity," as Anatole France ironically put it.

That led, in recent years, to the "starving in the midst of plenty" of so many millions. It led to the wholesale butchery of young men in the World War for victories that the survivors could not even hold in their hands and enjoy. It led to revolutions far more destructive than they were creative. The lowest level was reached with the totalitarian enterprises, building the power of a few national groups upon the enslavement of larger ones, who were more advanced in civic and spiritual civilization than their victors. It led to that grotesque exaltation of immedate efficiency, whereby dictators hoped to establish world domination (which is easy) and to maintain it (which is impossible) by taking into account everything except the fact that they were surrounded by hate and malediction.

The neglect and contempt for the human person have now brought forth all their fruits. The next epoch, the long and deep movements that will follow the turn of the tide, will start with man returning to man himself. I am not expressing a wish. I am foretelling an inevitable fact.

In our slightly worn-out vocabulary, this means revolution.

At this time, the reader may perceive that what I see growing ahead of us is revolution—whether we love or fear the idea.

But not one of these puny revolutions by which one class of people grabs the goods from another class, or destroys the goods altogether in the name of equality or something. And not one of these fake revolutions (the word being annexed because of its prestige) by which one or two empires upset the international balance of power, to their own profit.

I mean revolution within man himself which will leave him different from what he was.

Not just a rearranging of power and wealth between men. But a rearranging of man, of his own sense of right, of duty and of power. I mean his own.

In the world of today, it looks as though a crushing fatality, an enormous and truly inhuman curse make every one of us a victim of fate. Yet that fate is not the unpredictable work of unknown forces. It was manufactured by men. And not the best of men, at that.

They were allowed to play with our fate, to make our fate, because we did not keep it in our own hands.

The trend of material civilization is towards collective control of the world's resources, and distribution of its wealth with less and less privilege allowed to certain classes or nations. We knew that and we said so, without the help of the Nazis or the Bolsheviks. Redistribution of opportunities should take place without the suffering and destruction that are now imposed on innumerable people. But that is only one half of the picture. With everything concerning the mind, the soul, art, religion, or the simple expression of personality, from childhood to death, collective efficiency has nothing to do.

The laws of matter tend to unify the rules which men must accept. But spiritual life tends to diversify men. Public life demands discipline and a certain uniformity. Personal life cultivates the differences between men. Spiritual life makes each soul essentially different from all others—each one irreplaceable—and it is the very test and sign of a barbarous condition when men live in a confusion between what is and what is not of the soul. Fascism has carried that confusion to the extreme. And that is where it antagonizes Christianity, whose principal teaching is to render unto Caesar only that which is Caesar's.

The major result of the next revolution may be precisely this segregation of Caesar's realm, this drawing of a line around each man's personal domain, over which no one but himself should have authority, and where he can worship the gods of his own allegiance.

The little revolutions that have multiplied around us, and those which are suggested, do not interest me. Even those undertaken in the name of virtue and justice. That honest men, who may be corrupt tomorrow, should replace corrupt men who probably began by being honest, is not important. What we need is not more disorder, nor order at any price. It is a full civic education, and more faith in ourselves.

Conservatives are not bent on conserving what is best. They don't even know what is best. Revolutionists disappoint me, because I can foresee clearly that the drama they want to enact will not leave men very different. I demand more than that.

To take men, who doubt their own power, who accept evils which they could conquer, who make no use of their own genius, and to bring out their true selves—that is a revolution.

Christ did it with the soul of man and that is why his revolution has left the world different from what it was.

Because this world has been made intolerable for too many individuals, including some of the strongest, the bravest and the freest, revolution is bound to come. It will be of an entirely different kind from what we are used to.

It will take place, like the Christian revolution, where the tyrant cannot reach, and its effect will be to make this world a place where people can again live without having to part from their own souls.

A result of the present evil tide is the sweeping away of the small distinctions between men. Monarchists and republicans meet and discover that a decent king can rule a prosperous democracy. Philosophers and mystics are no longer interested in mutual excommunication.

The present time is full of horrible deeds and things. Yet I cannot hate the epoch I live in, because if the scandal is great, the promise is greater still. Men are wide awake at last. Their sin was to be inattentive. They resist and suffer, therefore they exist.

There used to be a very small number of people who understood what it meant to be alive in this age. There are millions now.

Nations disappear, forms of government become discredited, rulers rise and fall, the rich become poor and the poor do not become rich. So we put no longer our creed in slogans, our blind faith in human leaders, our confidence in luck or habit, nor our safety in numbers.

We shall have to recognize that the stuff which men are made of, and the use they make of that stuff, is what matters—in the end.

ON THE IMPORTANCE OF SEEING NEW THINGS WITH NEW EYES

This is not the time for crystal-gazing, they say.

This is the time for action. For taking care of the present.

All right. This book deals with the present. But there is more around us than most eyes can see. People are using their old eyes to look at new things. I do not mean new things to be, I mean the new things that are.

Agreed, this is a time for action. But it should not be blind action to be undone as fast as it is achieved. That is the way of inefficiency, waste and disaster. People indulge in action for action's sake, because it is much easier. It is only when all is going wrong and there is nothing left to do that they "stop and think."

But in our time, intelligence has been discredited as a result of too much intelligence being spent for worthless aims. Confronted with havoc, people blame intelligence.

When Hitler arose, people took too long before looking at him with the new eyes required by his new ideology and methods. When he embarked on his program, a small degree of attention would have shown he was wrong, and would have indicated how to cope with him. But people had done enough thinking by disapproving of him. So he succeeded, in spite of that disapproval. We had failed to measure his new methods with new eyes.

The concerted action against Hitler has finally triumphed along the very lines of unified planning which we refused to consider ten years ago. Let us not disturb anyone who is still engaged in that action. But let us not fail to see that it is those people who have risked the most, sacrificed the most and fought most continuously for the common cause, who also bring the clearest vision. That is why the Underground papers of Europe have supplied us with some of our most constructive ideas on Europe's future.

What if the time for decisive action were also the time for clear and ardent thinking, and for realistic prediction and planning?

It was the false prophets who discredited intelligence. The era which is just over belonged to them. They were of all kinds, some flattering, some violent, those who promised welfare, and those who demanded sacrifice (and they were the clever ones). They discredited sacrifice, too, by proving that it was easy to be had for ignoble aims. Hence the present world, which suggests those epochs mentioned in Genesis when God, confronted with His achievements, was seized with repentance.

Therefore, the ground should be ready for the true prophets. What is a prophet? A man inspired, who tells about the future? Yes, but let us look closer. First of all, it is a man with a profound knowledge of the present. Profound, in that he penetrates deeper than facts and figures, and discovers the seeds of a certain future—the promises and the threats of the seasons to come—things that cannot be perceived by those who grasp only the obvious.

The causes of to-morrow's events are already visible, but not to everyone. A prophet knows how yesterday's future has become the present. He knows that the present already contains more than one future, and that a choice is still possible.

Let us put it like this: the tree that will grow out of a seed planted today is not less real than that seed. The seed is present, hidden under the earth and the rotten leaves. Let a man stop and declare, in the midst of an open countryside: "Here a tree will grow." It is a purely rational operation, especially if the man himself has planted the seed. Every gardener is a prophet.

If a man stops at some river-bend, and declares: "Here a city shall grow"—especially if the land already is divided and allotted—that man is another minor prophet, as is any good speculator.

Now if he says: "Here a new God will have his temple," and if it is true, he must have a keen sense of his own epoch and of its aspirations. Yet the operation is not very different, except that he has dug deeper and recognized the presence of seeds of a subtler kind. Around us, at the present time, are seeds, some of which will become grass, others orchards, and others cathedrals.

Intelligent prevision should have appeared at the close of the last war when, for the first time in its history, the world attained its unity. A few people saw it and foresaw the consequences. But our creative political vision of 150 years ago had so deteriorated through a century of short-time efficiency and subrealism, that people did not realize how great the moment was. They were in a hurry to go back to their enclosures, to their safe deposits. And that unexploited, unperceived greatness left a whole generation with its thirst unquenched. Then came the villains, who exploited that thirst.

The impotence of democracies in making world democracy a success when the world belonged to them, left a whole generation with a taste of the unfinished, a sense of the discrepancy between past sacrifices and present results. Victorious democracy inflicted upon its believers their first deep disappointment, the spectacle of its own indolence after victory. What a temptation to let everything crack and crumble, to throw it all away! The dictators had an easy game of it. They had no competition. If instead of mediocre cheaters they had been true creators of a new order, that is, long-term realists, if instead of unethical politicians equipped with tricks and traps and big lies, they had been the bearers of some rich and fertile message, the world would have belonged to them. They almost succeeded in stealing it, but could not hold it.

Fascism and nazism are drugs to excite or console, not regimes to live by. They are an assemblage of what was left of ideas that used to be great, and of devotions gone to seed. That is the sign of the end of an era. With remnants of imperialism, bits of demagogy, memories of marxism, that hash was concocted—repellent food to a sound stomach. People cry for it insofar as they are sick; their minds crave it insomuch as they have lost confidence in their own power. Social classes that lean towards fascism are those which are already sentenced to die, and who feel it and call the devil to their help. What relation has it to the surge of real revolutions?

What fascism did to normal people was to provoke their normal elementary reflexes. Not economic, intellectual or partisan but human reflexes—the reflexes of a besieged city, of a shipwrecked crew, of a hunted man, of a starving man, of a man who is mad with anger. That brought them together, and that is where our story began.

When men, destitute and tortured, recognize each other and communion is discovered, then sometimes prophets arise. When souls are feverish and false idols lie shattered and yet faith is unconquered and pride is unbroken, then sometimes prophets arise. The mightiest one is not the most accurate, but the most passionate; he who contains such love and such hatred that all recognize in him what is deepest in them.

To people who are satiated and unconcerned, a prophet has no revelation to bring. He is a noisy and ridiculous intruder. At times when people are satisfied with their way of life, and incurious about the rest, all that a prophet can do is to trace a few flaming words on the wall, during a banquet. People stare and find the words cryptic. It frightens some and that is better than nothing.

But when a world is crashing down in fire and smoke, and men die by the thousands at the hands of other men, then new ideas appear among the strong. Ideas ready to take shape in words thundering and irresistible. Questions are asked, and strong men recognize one another by the manner in which they ask the questions. Questions raised by a whole world and addressed to a whole world, calling for answers that take in their stride a whole world's torment, despair, anger and hope.

I do not fear the absence of prophets in a near future.

I am afraid that there will be too many, and that people will flock too foolishly in their wake; that the loudest voices, not the highest inspiration, will triumph. I fear the worst—but only from the scared and immature, the lazy and irresponsible. I fear nothing from those who have survived danger and loneliness, with their eyes wide open, who have crossed beyond despair with their courage intact.

These are the makers of a revolution, which is of a new kind. A revolution which I believe *has already taken place,* only the news of it is not in the papers. A revolution that did not happen on the streets but inside the souls of men, where every cause has its beginning and its end, where the seed of every action is born and dies.

What has taken place in ten countries of Europe is a return of man to his own soul, reborn and fiercely tempered by four years of concentration on things fundamental. Possessions, happiness, safety had all vanished in smoking destruction, and there was nothing left of man's heritage but that tragic domain, that devastated garden which is enclosed within the walls of his body and of his mind, yet is as great as the universe.

And there remained, throughout the years of darkness, what can be neither absorbed nor conquered, any more than Rome in her glory could control the solitary soul of a slave, clinging to his new creed . . .

This is not a book of prophesies. It deals with actual facts. It is not like Jefferson predicting the establishment of democracy, or Marx announcing the advent of communism, or de Gaulle foreseeing motorized warfare, or Jules

Verne opening new vistas to scientific imagination and prefiguring the inventions to come.

It is more like a pamphlet written around the year 1400 to say that the earth is round.

That is not prophecy.

It's just plain heresy.

NOTES

1. EUROPE: POPULATION FIGURES
(In Millions)

Nations	In Europe	Other countries bordering on the Mediterranean Sea (Greater Europe)	Under European allegiance (dominions, colonies, mandates, etc.)
France	42	French North Africa, Syria and Lebanon...20	French Empire or federation....52
Poland	32		
Yugoslavia	15.7		
Czechoslovakia	15.2		
Netherlands	8.8		Netherlands Empire......61
Belgium	8.3		Belgian Congo...10
Greece	7.1		
Denmark	3.8		
Norway	2.8		
Luxembourg	.3		
Total for the "10 liberated nations"	136	20	123
England	48	Palestine........2	British dominions and Colonies..102
			India..........388
Russia (in Europe)	129		Russia in Asia....42
Total for the 12 United Nations of Europe	313	22	655

Nations	In Europe	Other countries bordering on the Mediterranean Sea (Greater Europe)	Under European allegiance (dominions, colonies, mandates, etc.)
Spain	26	Spanish Morocco.. 1	
Austria	6.8		
Albania	1.2		
Portugal	6.3		Portuguese Colonies 10
Sweden	6.3		
Switzerland	4.3		
Eire	2.9		
Turkey (in Europe)	1.2	Turkey in Asia....17 Egypt...........16	
Lithuania, Latvia, Estonia	6		
Total for the intermediary category	61	34	10
Italy	44	Libya 1	
Roumania	18		
Hungary	9		
Bulgaria	6.4		
Finland	3.6		
Total for the Axis ex-satellites	81	1	
Germany (1937)	66		
TOTAL	521	57	665

These figures (corresponding to pre-war Europe) are from the *Political Handbook of the World* and from *Europe*, an atlas by Marthe Rajchman (1944).

War losses, migrations and deportations have modified substantially these figures, and they will be further affected by territorial changes after the war, and by the differences in birth-rate.

These figures are not given, therefore, as an accurate evaluation of Europe's demography of tomorrow, but as a basis for such evaluation.

It will be noted that the "10 liberated nations" include about 26% of the total population of Europe proper, England 9% and Russia 25%. *Together they form 60% of the total.* With Spain, Austria, Albania and the neutrals, a federated Europe would start with 72% of the total population. Of the 28% remaining, 15% are the former Axis satellites and 13% are the Germans.

It may be noticed also that the total population of countries either belonging to Greater Europe or having allegiance to European nations, is 1243 million, that is, 57.28% of the total world population. 2170 million

Principal clusters of population in the world are:

```
Europe (with Mediterranean shores)........578 million
China ................................450      "
India ................................388      "
North America (U.S., Canada and Mexico)....165   "
```

2. THE WAY OF ALL CONQUEST

TWO ATTEMPTS AT EMPIRE

History does not repeat itself. Yet certain political cycles have a way of recurring. For example a weak or corrupt democracy drifts into demagogy, which leads to dictatorship, therefore tyranny, which breeds rebellion, which brings back democracy. Any regime is full of prestige and appeal for people who are unhappy under the opposite regime.

Twice in 130 years, Europe was conquered and subjugated for a brief period and each time by one man. There is such an amazing parallel and also such a contrast between Napoleon and Hitler, that by looking at both adventures there is a fair chance of detecting the constant elements—the inevitable steps in the way of all conquest.

It is easy enough to show how different the man Hitler is

from the man Bonaparte, yet the graphs of their lives, within certain limits, are strikingly similar. Each started from nothing became dictator by riding on the crest of a revolutionary wave commanded the best military machine of his time and used it to conquer Europe.

The rise of Napoleon, from 1793 to 1808, was a swift and miraculous adventure: in less than fifteen years, the unknown and penniless artillery captain had become an emperor, ruler of Europe, and a "brother" of the remaining sovereigns who crowded meekly around him. Yet his fall was even more spectacular. In the summer of 1812, his power over the Continent was undisputed and no one seemed able to resist his will. In the summer of 1814, he had lost everything, was exiled to the Island of Elba, and France was left smaller than he had found her.

We shall not retrace the Fuehrer's career to his position as dominator of continental Europe. Events of these last years are sufficiently present to our memories: the political rise of Hitler in Germany at a time of acute economic depression, weak leadership and popular despondency; his access to power, legitimized by various plebiscites. Then the rearmament of Germany, the political alignment with Italy, the joint intervention in Spain, the seizure of Austria, the breaking up of Czechoslovakia at Munich, the subsequent violation of the Munich agreement through the occupation of Prague, the deal with Russia, the joint conquest of Poland, the seizure of Denmark and the conquest of Norway, the invasion of Holland and Belgium, the victory over France and, in 1941, the conquest of the whole Balkan peninsula. Such were the steps to a complete military control of the European Continent. The few countries that were still unoccupied knew that their independence could be canceled by Hitler at a moment's notice if it were to his interest or his whim. The European situation in 1941 was much the same as that of 1812. Leaving aside generalities, let us now draw a list of those definite points which are in common between the Napoleonic conquest and the Hitlerian one.

1. The dictator seizes power, following disorder and inefficiency under the previous regime, which has fallen into discredit. Pessimism is replaced by hope, expressed in plebiscites following the dictator's successful coup.

2. The totalitarian state. Suppression of political opposition in any form. The police force becomes one of the main instruments of government.

3. Distrust of the church as a rival power. Efforts to subordinate the church to the state. As a result, a growing number of people come to regard the dictator as a power of evil.

4. Everything for the army. It becomes rapidly the best in Europe. From general to private, it enjoys a high standing and prestige (rather than material privileges) above anything it could hope for under another regime. Therefore it has everything to lose from a change and will support the dictator to the bitter end.

5. A few men on top receive rich material rewards.

6. Efficiency and speed in all enterprises. In foreign policy, everything sacrificed to short-term results; the use of terror, unscrupulousness, disregard for treaties and the pledged word. Success is largely due to violation of all existing rules. This is called gangsterism by the dictator's enemies. His partisans call it realism.

7. The conquest of Europe is accomplished through a series of separate aggressions against one power at a time, while the others are unprepared and unwilling to interfere. (The conqueror's country has the largest single population in Europe, outside of Russia.)

8. A measure of support is found in each country in the social classes which are dissatisfied with existing regimes and hope to gain by a change. In the early 19th century, these were the popular, unprivileged classes hoping to destroy traditional

monarchy and aristocracy. To-day, it is the privileged groups hoping to break the trend toward the left.

9. Occupation of most of the Continent, following a succession of military victories. The dictator's popularity with his own nation reaches unprecedented heights. Paris, Berlin, Vienna, Warsaw, Rome, and Madrid are garrisoned by the dictator or by his satellites.

10. War is made profitable by high-pressure exploitation of conquered lands, whose resources are literally plundered to feed, supply, and enrich the conquerors.

11. The populations conquered are at first half resigned, then become angry and restless. Disappointed appeasers turn against the conqueror.

12. Failure to control the seas. Need to defeat England by invasion or blockade, yet being blockaded by her fleets. England suffers economically, but keeps the mastery of the sea, huge reserves of wealth, and an inflexible will to resist. She sends only small armies to the Continent, but remains the headquarters of European rebellion against the dictator.

13. Temporary agreement with Russia. The Russian autocrat realizes, however, that a complete triumph of the dictator would reduce Russia to the part of a satellite, or worse. In the meantime, the two powers exchange services, divide spheres of influence in Eastern Europe, and devise plans for a common conquest of the Near East and Western Asia.

14. Attempt to raise the meaning of the empire to that of a New Order, and failure to persuade the people concerned that this is not just an afterthought.

15. The hopelessness of appeasement. In spite of all their motives for resistance, people and nations might have paid any price for peace. But the actions of the dictator convinced them that no matter how high the price, the bargain would not stand and a higher price would be demanded almost immediately. It became a certainty that the nations would have to

pay with everything they had—and get no peace. Thus the spirit of unconquerable resistance grew in the hearts of millions of people who had lived as confirmed pacifists hitherto, and the time came when no peace talk or peace offer coming from the dictator could any longer find credit.

16. After a period of more or less sincere collaboration, the dictator invades Russia with a powerful army.

17. The campaign becomes longer and costlier than the conqueror had expected, he fails to reach his major objectives, and the campaign ends in humiliating retreat.

18. The coalition becomes a crusade. The master of Europe faces invasion from all sides . . .

Differences between the two careers are too easy to point out. Some circumstances have facilitated Hitler's task.

The difficulties of armed rebellion to-day are obvious. A century ago, a determined group of Spanish or Tyrolian rebels could fight regular troops with almost equal weapons. A riot, or fighting from behind barricades, could hold a garrison in check. To-day tanks, machine-guns and planes make rebellion far more desperate. Besides, the technique of political police, espionage and repression have made progress.

However, Napoleon was not defeated by popular uprisings. The threat of them obliged him to garrison many places with troops which he could have put to better use, just as the threat of disorder throughout Europe immobilized a growing portion of Germany's manpower and war material. But popular movements became really important only after the dictator had been defeated in war.

On the other hand, there was a tremendous difference in the civic and national maturity of conquered peoples in 1812 and in 1942, which told against Hitler's prospects of ever winning acceptance of his rule. In Napoleon's time, a vast number of people had no idea of national allegiance beyond the duty to obey their king. Although some free and proud people were ready to fight a foreign invader, the indifferent masses, in Germany for instance, did not feel any particular offense at being conquered. In many places, the French administration brought a definite betterment to existing conditions, greater facilities for popular education, etc. Hitler brings nothing of the sort. Europeans, in our time, having known national independence and practiced free institutions, are far more reluctant to accept a foreign and undemocratic ruler than their ancestors were in 1810.

Napoleon raised a large number of troops from the conquered lands. Most of these people fought very well for him. Besides the Poles who were actual allies of Napoleon, fighting for the resurrection of their nation he had in his Great Army of 1812 of about 600,000 men, some 300,000 foreigners, 200,000 of which were Germans. The Bavarian cavalry gave an excellent account of itself at the battle of Borodino. It was the Bavarians who suppressed the Tyrolian revolt of 1809. The Poles and Mamelukes were used in Spain. The Italians fought at Smolensk.

But the troops that Hitler squeezed from his satellites had no feeling of loyalty to him.

Whatever sincerity, or lack of it, Napoleon himself may have placed at the service of democratic principles, there was a universal appeal in the French Revolution and he benefited by it. That appeal was totally lacking in the German-Nazi revolution. The first revolution was rational and world-wide in its principles. The latter is racial and national. Military efficiency could be achieved in the service of either, but the dynamism in the "propagation of the faith" was colossal in the first case, in the second it is nil. Nazism can win paid servants, intimidate millions, create imitators and evoke appeasers. It cannot win sincere foreign enthusiasts to Hitler's person or program. Nazism might have become universal as a de facto rule. By definition, it cannot be anything but German in its nature and principle.

A last element should be mentioned about Hitlerian Germany. Although it may appear unimportant to some "realists," yet no one at this point can tell how heavily it has counted against the prestige of the Nazi New Order. It is the divorce from free culture.

A few people of talent, such as Benjamin Constant and Madame de Staël, chose to live outside of France during the reign of Napoleon. But most scientists, artists, and teachers remained where they lived and carried on with their work without interference. It would not have occurred to Goethe or to Beethoven to leave their homeland and to go into exile because the French had defeated their sovereign and occupied their country. Free political opposition was suppressed, it is true, but cultural life went on very much undisturbed, both in France and in the countries conquered. Napoleon was not so totalitarian that the teaching of music or painting, or even history, all over Europe, had to conform to the dictates of "Chambers of Culture" such as existed in Nazi Germany. Besides, Napoleon had scientific culture, expressed himself with remarkable soberness and precision, and even had a sense of humor. French soldiers, therefore, were not ordered to burn the books of Chateaubriand or Kant. In spite of imperial discipline, France could still boast of being a center of the arts and sciences.

3. THE FUTURE THAT WAS

When General Pershing landed with the first American units at Boulogne in 1917, he was greeted by a French general who commanded the northern region and whose name was Dumas. I know nothing about him except that he said the following:

"Your coming opens a new era in the history of the world. The United States of America is now taking its part with the United States of Europe. Together they are about to found the United States of the World, which will definitely and finally end the war and give a peace which will be enduring, and fruitful for mankind."

At the time, people must have thought that General Dumas was eloquent. Later, they would have called him optimistic. History will simply say that he was accurate, because history takes a long view of things, and when the above prediction comes true, it will appear that world unity was born precisely when America joined hands with Europe in a common cause.

For the first time in the history of men, the largest part of mankind was engaged in the same task. The fact that a majority was fighting on one side and a minority on the other side, is not what matters. What matters is that for the first time, so many human beings were affected at the same time by the same events.

There is something instructive, historically speaking, in the general's words. It is the fact that to most Europeans, at the time of the "coming of the Yanks," hopes were widespread and well founded. The masses believed that American cooperation, and eventually American leadership, had a purpose beyond the clinching of military victory for the Allies. It was the declared purpose to make the world safe for democracy, to organize international peace on a realistic basis of collective assistance against aggression. It did not occur to Europe that three years later America would withdraw suddenly from all cooperation, wreck the house for which she had drafted the plans, and change into skepticism or despair the reasonable expectations that had been aroused, and all this merely because it was election year. I assume that after twenty-five years, these things can be said frankly.

Yet America's withdrawal was not sufficient to destroy the

international enterprise. That enterprise managed to grow and even to succeed, for twelve more years.

What happened, and what most observers failed to observe, was the first awakening of international ethics, or rather the emergence of ethical rules applied to world statesmanship.

There was little that was "idealistic" or disinterested about this innovation. The plain, hard and realistic facts in the case were that war did not pay, that no nation was strong enough to face a world coalition and that any war anywhere was a threat to everybody.

So the nations agreed to limit their hitherto unbounded sovereignty by accepting some elementary rules of behavior, including renunciation of the free use of force. Vast majorities of opinion in civilized countries had reached the conclusion that a minimum of moral law was indispensable not only within national communities, but even between them—a new turn of thought. And so we embarked on this new experiment, the League. It must be admitted that few people, even among those who participated in the experiment, had a clear grasp of the fact that this was the most important moment in the whole history of man.

Outlawing war was not the product of a definite school of thought or of one man's influence. Woodrow Wilson formulated what millions had expected. Men did not become suddenly unselfish, but success became a different proposition. For instance, in Western Europe, a statesman who would have won popular applause thirty years earlier by exalting conquest won the same applause by extolling arbitration. Human nature had not been transformed in thirty years. But conquest no longer seemed profitable. The man of 1919 was beginning to extend to international behavior the elementary rules of ethics which had proved serviceable within the city or the nation. And he did so because the total absence of international ethics had led to costly failure.

This was the true motive for everything constructive in the peace treaties of 1919: the setting up of the first world-wide society of nations, the provisions for peaceful revision of treaties, the protection of minorities, the mandate system, the International Labor Organization—to note only some of the features that made these peace treaties different from any others in history. Politics in America, and German propaganda the world over, caused public attention to focus on the shortcomings of the Treaty. Everybody came to hear about them. Even today, a vast number of educated, responsible people have not yet taken the trouble to read the twenty-six short articles of the League Covenant. But it does not keep these people from passing judgment on the League and the Treaty.

A few weeks after the armistice of 1918, the President of the United States came to Europe and brought the full force, both moral and material, of the most powerful country in the world to the service of one cause—the cause of lasting peace.

Our people—I say our *people*—knew so well what the President was standing for, and their hopes were so great, that when he arrived in Paris among my countrymen—my skeptical, mocking and proud countrymen—many of them were seen to kneel down in the street as he passed by.

Men who came back from the war had one idea in their heads: "Everything that can be done or attempted, should be done or attempted, so that our children should not have to live through what we have had to endure." And what millions of Frenchmen wanted and hoped for at that time, millions of Englishmen, Germans, Italians, and millions from many other nations also wanted.

One year later, physical collapse and the destructive work of politics both at home and abroad made Woodrow Wilson appear as a defeated leader, a man whose ideas were discarded, whose inspiration was rejected, whose leadership was a thing of the past.

There was much talk, in 1920, of the League of Nations being dead, dead and finished with and buried under the overwhelming vote which carried a new president to the White House. In Europe we did not realize very clearly what was happening. But an immense disappointment fell on the people of the world. No greater backward step was ever taken, than this retreat of our nations to their local policies, their local hostilities, their local fears.

During these years a handful of men were at work keeping alive the League of Nations. They had almost no support; even many friends of peace deserted them because the League was not exactly the kind of League they had wanted, and because it did not instantly crystallize all their ideals. We worked without the support of those great men with world-wide authority who were contented with criticizing the League's imperfections. I must mention this desertion of the League by those who were best qualified to help it with public opinion. Conscientious objectors are respectable, but there is one man who has a right to speak harshly to the conscientious objector, and that is the stretcher-bearer.

We pulled through several dangerous years. The fact that sixty nations subscribed to the Covenant, and that fifty-seven of them lived up to its principles in their behavior during 20 years, is enough to show that American leadership of 1919 had brought fruit—in spite of the American politics of 1920.

It was during the winter of 1923–24 that in France, Germany and England, public opinion began to demand that we should put our theories more vigorously into practice and give the new ethics a chance to materialize, and world institutions an opportunity to prove their usefulness.

I shall never forget the reasonable enthusiasm that inspired our League of Nations groups in France, during that winter when we created the "Comité d'Action" to coordinate the scattered efforts of university groups, ex-service men, writers, experts, and those of the pacifists who had enough realism in them to seek the efficient means of making war more difficult, or impossible.

After 1923, the international organizations picked up and managed to grow. The merit lies with the masses in Europe, their horror of war and their capacity for generous support of a constructive idea, and with the untiring work of a few statesmen, a few writers, a few League of Nations civil servants. The rest of the world was, at best, mildly skeptical or distrustful. Communists and "society" were hostile, for different reasons.

The work was carried on under such leaders as Briand, Stresemann, Cecil, Beneš, and with the help of anonymous millions who supported them: ex-service men of France and Germany, women, students, labor, religious groups from everywhere. Those who helped can pride themselves today on having put their common sense and their devotion at the service of such a cause.

Since then, all great leaders of public thought have been awakened to their responsibilities. Their awakening came after Hitler rose to power. It came when they realized that not only freedom, the dignity of man, but the very possibility of culture were being wrecked for the sake of political efficiency by totalitarian regimes. I shall not include the amateurish and irresponsible "liberals" who were capable only of damning the faults of the League, and never shared in our positive efforts. Either peace would come, without their having done much for it, or war, without their having done anything useful against it.

HOW WE FAILED

We of the Western democracies need to investigate more closely the puzzling fact of our obvious weakness in the face of the dictatorial bullying between 1935 and 1939. What was the real nature of our inferiority? Was this inferiority the result of subservience and passivity inherent to our regimes? Of our pacifism or of our good living? Was it temporary, or final?

The effect would have been the same had we been utterly disorganized as groups and degenerate as individuals. Yet I believe that the colossal handicap in favor of the aggressors was due to this: their methods were exactly adapted to a period of trouble and disorder, whereas ours applied successfully to peace, but not to those five years (1934 to 1939) of emergency without war.

Our ways and rules are conceived for normal and peaceful times. In war, we set aside our individual rights and privileges. We had fought and won a great war, during which compulsion, secrecy, regimentation in all its forms, were a necessity. That made us hate war even more. The moment the war was over, we resumed our democratic ways with immense relief. It is a fact that not a single one of our victorious generals played any conspicuous part in our public affairs as soon as peace was restored, whereas the defeated generals of Germany became in several cases her peacetime leaders. When we are at peace, we are at peace and live accordingly.

The totalitarian regimes, being always at war, figuratively or actually, against something or other—communism or Jewry or the rich or the foreigners or pacifism or religion or ordinary decency or some other enemy—maintain a war mentality in peacetime, which is the principal secret of their success. They use war methods without waiting for actual war; this gives them an immense advantage over us. They regiment their own people, conscripting them with or without compensation, as we do only in time of war but as they do all the time. Desperate or brutal measures become quite in order, since war permits them. We did not retaliate because we were at peace. They could suppress public discussion of their policies, as a requirement of the emergency which they themselves created when it did not exist.

Dictators are like sea-captains claiming a life-and-death authority over their crew and passengers on account of the extreme peril in which the ship finds itself—after they had steered the ship into the most dangerous waters precisely in order to impose that kind of authority.

In a time of disorder without war, our regimes are at a great disadvantage, being handicapped in their foreign policies by internal opposition, public indifference, panicky moves engineered by the demagogues, and the like. As a result, we were constantly outmaneuvered.

The people, who have the sovereignty, exert it only in a negative way when they make clear that they do not want this or that. The rest of the time, it is a frozen sovereignty. Our people know their duties in time of war, but few of them are familiar with their responsibility in the conduct of national and foreign affairs in normal times.

Their information, however, had progressed quite actively in the last decade. It had proceeded, in America, from the educated classes down, but had not yet reached the masses. It had proceeded in Europe from the masses up, and a large portion of the ruling classes did not participate in it. The cause of this contrast is to be found largely in the fact that European masses were more directly acquainted with war, and had done their thinking about it.

On the whole, public opinion was very nearly ready to take an intelligent stand on world affairs. In such unofficial consultations as the "Peace Ballot" taken in England in 1935, the public showed a far greater degree of discrimination than some of the editorials would have led us to believe. Many newspapers underestimated the demand of their readers for intelligent material.

But world conditions required more than just the outspoken

expression of a "vigorous" stand by our people on such international issues as the Jewish persecutions, the Japanese cruelties, or the massacre of 12,000 Spanish children by air raids. A mere stand does no good if it is not implemented. The atrocities I refer to have been perpetrated not once, but as a continuous policy for several years, while a near-unanimity of our people disapproved of them, to say the least, and publicized their censure in every way. As soon as the offenders became assured that we would stop short of any action, such as effective economic measures, they went ahead very much undisturbed.

Why did we stop at a mere barrage of words, or shouts of indignation?

Because in our system, a strong expression of approval or blame, by a majority, is practically an act. It is enough to make the law or change it. Within our borders, it is impossible for anyone to run counter to the whole of public opinion once it has been aroused. But internationally, that ceases to be true.

As a result, there was something naive and pathetic in the pained surprise of our people who found that their usual methods did not function; that their voices were not listened to; that our majority rule did not work on Mr. Hitler or General Franco; that the will of our people was of no special concern to Mr. Mussolini or General Araki. They discovered with real amazement and chagrin, that honest thinking and liberal intent are not enough to constitute a policy. And that an aggressor who has made up his mind to run the terrible risks of war and who accepts and imposes temporary impoverishment of his people in order to get what he wants, is not going to change his mind because a number of benevolent foreigners let him know that they disapprove of his course.

As a matter of fact, much of the contempt and mockery in which totalitarians indulged in regard to us, was based on our impotent blaming of their successful activities. They regarded it as amateurish and frivolous, nor did they understand why we took so much trouble to pass judgment on policies and events which did not concern us directly. They felt uneasy because after all it might suddenly occur to us to do something about it. But as long as we did not, the weather was fine and the path was clear.

Other nations, forced to adopt a defensive attitude, did not act in a concerted manner, except for a common Franco-British foreign policy which was sometimes hard to achieve. That was the case when the Spanish war broke out and led to a purely negative compromise, the non-intervention policy, which became a painful farce in view of the resolute intervention of Germany and Italy.

Besides, there being many shades of opinion, the easiest course for democratic governments was naturally to do nothing in order not to antagonize any group of voters.

The choice before the fifty-odd non-totalitarian nations was apparently between abject capitulation and unorganized, desperate resistance which would make each one a separate, easy victim for the aggressors.

So there was, obviously, a contradiction between our theories and our practice, between our principles and our behavior in foreign affairs. Was the trouble with the theory or with the practice?

A good example is what happened after the World Economic Conference of 1927. It included all the members of the League, plus such non-members as the United States and the Soviet Union. It reached, believe it or not, unanimous conclusions as to what nations could do and especially as to what they should not do in regard to international trade and the ultimate prosperity of each and all. The men who arrived at these conclusions were selected by fifty governments, presumably with a view to future guidance in the economic policies of their respective nations.

The curious thing is that after the conference these same nations engaged merrily in doing just what their own delegates had agreed to be disastrous, and abstained from practicing what had been advocated. They did it on grounds of immediate expediency, hoping that the future would take care of itself. The future was the greatest economic depression in the world's history.

What our nations did in regard to the preservation and enforcement of peace was on the same lines. The best example is our behavior in the Far East conflict. Everyone in the League, except Siam, condemned the Japanese aggression and found it detrimental to our interests. When the League passed a strong resolution denouncing it in October 1937, the American State Department within twenty-four hours issued a declaration stating complete approval of the League's resolution. Then the Japanese were allowed to proceed, and we embarked upon selling them something like 80%—the United States alone supplying 56%—of what they needed to carry on the war.

Few people denied that if and when Japan won the war in China, the Western nations would lose:

1. The surplus trade consisting in war supplies, the need for them being over.

2. Most of their previous trade, because Japan would have acquired permanently much of the needed sources of supplies.

3. Their trade with China, where their industries would be supplanted by Japanese industries with a vast market under their exclusive control.

4. A number of other markets, where Japanese trade based on cheap Chinese labor regimented and organized by Japan, and supported by Japanese diplomacy and armed force, would undersell and chase out Western producers incapable of competing.

Few people denied this, although many "had not thought about it." But most of them just rejoiced in the momentary boom in exports, and simply refused to take a further view of coming events.

Most people, who would think in terms of ten or fifteen years in evaluating the prospective returns of an investment, or the cost-versus-profit of building a new bridge, would feel (not even think) their way in terms of the next six months in regard to the foreign policy of their country.

This state of irresponsibility is not the result of a conflict between ideals and vital interests. It is not, as André Siegfried said about many Frenchmen, a case of having "one's heart on the left and one's pocket-book on the right." Our vital interests were tied to the principles of international behavior that we set up in 1919. A cynic would say that this is precisely why we had formulated them. We had everything to gain by enforcing peace, not to speak of spiritual and cultural preservation. We had nothing to gain, and a good deal to risk, by allowing war to be restored as an instrument of national policy. We disregarded and deserted our principles for no profit, at the risk of losing our trade, our security, our independence. We permitted, if not actually helped, nations to behave again like outlaws. We, who welcomed international ethics, let them relapse into the primitive stage. We were the losers at this game.

Enforcement of peace, through the successful working of international machinery, had come very near to becoming a reality. But each time a concerted policy was required, one of us happened to desert or to straggle behind. The principle was clear enough. As early as May 27, 1916, Senator Henry Cabot Lodge wrote the following lines:

"If we are to promote international peace at the close of the present terrible war, if we are to restore international law as it must be restored, we must find some way in which the united forces of the nations could be put behind the cause of peace and law."

Only four years later, that principle was set aside because Mr. Wilson had said the same things, and it was less important to save world peace than to defeat the Democratic party.

For years, French opinion supported steadily the principle of collective security, and France, with the small nations grouped around her, was ahead of other great nations in accepting and advocating the application of sanctions against an aggressor (Geneva Protocol, 1924). Yet a large part of French opinion and of the French press wavered and deserted when the time came to stop the Italian aggression of 1935. As a result, the small nations abandoned the French system of security.

The British elected and supported a government which engineered the Munich surrender and allowed the destruction of Spanish democracy. As a result, many British ships have been sunk since 1939.

What we do not realize yet is that we, the people, are entirely to blame. Official policies are only the expression of what most of the people will support. The people cannot be flattered any longer into believing that they are always right, virtuous, peaceful and liberal and that our wicked governments are the villains. Nor should we get the credit for peace, and our leaders get the blame for the dangers. The dangers were born of our own short-mindedness, absent-mindedness, or intellectual cowardice. The mistakes and desertions of our leaders were nothing but our own.

4. THE AWAKENING

1918 to 1938. That was only yesterday.
We based the rules of our international club on the prin-

ciple that all of us were going to behave like gentlemen. That is, not to hold up a fellow-member if we met him alone in a dark street. Out of sixty, some fifty-seven of us did behave like gentlemen. That is a consoling fact. We know by now that this is not enough.

With the Manchurian and Ethiopian wars, the clock was set back thirty years.

With the persecution of liberal thought and expression, it was set back one hundred years.

With the persecution of Jews it was set back two hundred years or more.

With the rebuilding of the Germanic-Roman Empire, including Spain and extending its shadow over Latin America, we were back in the sixteenth century.

This was getting more and more interesting. There are a number of thrilling events, some of them very much to the credit of our forefathers, that used to be buried in the history of past generations. These events are ahead of us once more, for us and our children to enact.

It was so comfortable. At regular intervals, we lulled ourselves back into pious slumber with a speech, a patriotic song, a reference to immortal principles, to the Minute Men, to the Bastille.

The Bastille . . . Well, we took it, didn't we?

That one, yes. Took it and destroyed it, on the 14th of July 1789.

(But look around. The world is alive with Bastilles all around. Plenty of them, to be taken and to be destroyed.)

We kept rubbing our eyes.

Aggressions? Yes, far away. Manchuria, Ethiopia. Who ever goes there?

Then, gradually, it came closer. Madrid and Prague. We had to wake up.

How harmless, how nice and incongruous, the brave, exaggerated words of our national anthems, "And the flag was still there." "Contre nous, de la tyrannie, l'étendard sanglant est levé," when the schoolchildren sang it together, in July.
"Ils viennent jusque dans nos bras
Egorger nos fils, nos compagnes"
What do you say? It is exactly what German and Italian planes have been doing in Spain?
Why, yes. It is exactly what they have been doing.
It was so unreal when the children sang it. But so many children will not sing it any more.

That old Marseillaise. "A song that made tyrants tremble in their shoes"—once.

(Written in the Spring of 1939.)

5. FROM "NOTES TO MY FRIENDS" (1940–1941)

[*These "Notes" were sent to American friends in 1940 and 1941, at the time of our greatest disasters. My purpose in quoting from them is to show that the basic ideas of this book were expressed at a time when to most people Europe appeared doomed to German domination. America was neutral, and still remote from international responsibilities. Five years have demonstrated that these ideas were not over-optimistic; just "premature"—as people said then.*]

June 23, 1940

The war begins.
I mean the world war.
The European war might have ended with an Allied victory, with every nation keeping its independence or seeing it

restored. A German victory cannot bring peace to Europe, because the nature of each German victory is to enslave more people and make them irreconcilable.

Seventy million Germans and their vassals cannot keep a whole continent enslaved. Other continents are now wide awake to the fate which will be theirs if Germany is allowed to have her way. The small nations of Europe had no illusions about German rule, but they were powerless and without common leadership. The French were divided about the gravity of the Nazi peril. The British took a long time to realize its deadliness. But today the whole world knows that Germany *cannot* stop short of ruling the entire planet, and the planet *cannot* accept Germany's rule.

Either the British Empire, aided by the remaining forces of its Allies and by new support, will break Germany's effort and the nightmare will be over, or Germany will conquer England, and something new will begin: a long, unceasing world rebellion. Such a rebellion will not come from the dictation of leaders but will spring from the depths of individuals; and it will not abate until Germany has been defeated and disarmed.

In the first event, victory may come comparatively soon, if enough forces are mobilized immediately so that Germany becomes exhausted before achieving her world conquest.

In the second case, the rebellion is likely to be long-lived, since the necessary process of achieving world unity against oppression will have to be carried on under oppression. Yet other empires have been destroyed before, and the *final* result is what matters.

Resignation to German rule? Acceptance of German "superiority"?

If the superior mechanized organization of Germany triumphs over its present enemies, and runs the world, *who* actually will be ruling over two billion unwilling people? A horde of politicians, bureaucrats, Prussian generals, and police officials, together with the few young men who survive, who will be tired and disgusted with war, as were the victors of 1918, and a host of foreign hirelings who will not even enjoy the confidence of their Nazi masters.

Can we imagine the world under that domination? We have to, because it may well happen, if the British Empire does not defeat Hitler now. Do we imagine that such a domination could last? I don't, but I think of the price we shall have to pay if we choose the slow way.

The choice is between three issues:
1. To submit, and to become the have-nots in a world where the Nazi will be master.
2. To unite immediately under Anglo-American leadership, and to put all available resources of every kind into the fight against a conqueror whose plans are not ready to cope with such a new coalition.
3. To engage in the slower and costlier process of piecemeal and divided rebellion *after* the Nazis win. That will be the only course left if we refuse the other two.

In Europe, west of Russia, the Germans are only one-fifth of the population. In the whole world they are one-thirtieth. Is the trouble with the subdued majority the fact that it is made up of nations and people, some of whom eat too much and others not enough? Maybe. The fact is, 90% of the people, disunited and terrorized, are about to be ruled by a force that is not even composed of the best. Just a gang with a purpose.

The question now is whether 90% of mankind can agree on a purpose, or whether they must drift into slavery out of absent-mindedness.

July 9, 1940

A word to the friends of France, whose deep and warm understanding is doing so much to strengthen our passionate confidence in the future of our country, regardless of victories and defeats. A nation that inspires love of such quality and force is indeed a nation rich with undying promises.

There is a great deal of noise in the world, about the success of empires which take men and make them into slaves. All over the same world, however, there are people who suffer and hope for France, whose destiny was to take slaves and make them into men.

We underestimated material forces. It would be a grave mistake, now, to underestimate spiritual forces.

A faith and a love dependent upon military success would not deserve respect. But disaster can serve a useful purpose, by forcing us to clarify our faith and to concentrate our allegiance upon what is permanent and indestructible.

In the past, empires that overstretched their limits crumbled to pieces. Do you remember that together we smashed four of them, twenty-one years ago? But France survives, the nation and her people. And in a reasonable, yet tough and incorruptible fidelity to her own course, she has always found the secret of how to keep close to the true nature of man.

I feel that it is for us to console and fortify those friends of France who pay too much attention to the daily bad news and to desperate prophecies. Yes the situation seems desperate. It has been desperate more than once in our past. Of course the weak and the tired will lose courage and submit. We have other things to do than to pass judgment on them.

The thing we must not do is to emulate those who defeated us. If we have been lacking in modern methods of information, disciplined coordination, and faithfulness to our own principles, it does not follow that we should put our hopes in German information, Prussian discipline, and the Nazi forms of service.

It is within ourselves, and through knowledge and use of the best in ourselves, that we must discover the foundations for our new enterprises, and in our old virtues the seed of future power.

Such power as others can neither steal nor destroy.

Summer of 1941
(From a pamphlet on the Free French Forces)
What do the French people feel, want, hope?
The French are now distributed as follows:

1. Prisoners of war—about one and one half million.

2. In occupied France, under German rule—over twenty-five million.

3. In unoccupied France, under the Vichy regime and in the overseas territories under Vichy rule—about fifteen million (including the refugees from occupied France).

4. In Free French colonies, in the British Empire and in neutral countries.

As the distribution of the French in these various sections is largely a result of the circumstances of the war, the opinions of those who are free to express themselves may be taken to represent and reveal what exists also in the minds and hearts of Frenchmen under enemy occupation or control.

The prisoners of war, who are a large part of the young male population, are not in a position to make their voices heard. But is it difficult to imagine how they feel about a possible British victory that would set them free?

Living close to the enemy and suffering daily from his presence, the French in occupied France are in a vast majority opposed to collaboration.

In the unoccupied part of France, we have definite means of knowing what the masses think, in the letters sent freely or smuggled at a risk, and in the testimony of visitors. Voluntary collaboration with the enemy is confined to an exceedingly small class of people, although forced submission and inarticulate resignation must exist.

In a free and neutral country such as the United States, an overwhelming majority is "Free French," whether or not people have actually joined organized associations.

We can truly assume that the Free French represent a majority feeling of France. For every three men who join de Gaulle, probably thirty have tried and failed—some will try again. The proportion varies, of course. There are villages in Brittany where the whole population moved to England while it was still possible, rather than stay under German occupation. Such emigration is impossible today, but every sign shows that between those who stay and those who succeed in leaving, the difference is not one of opinion but of opportunity.

Nothing could be more unfair and more untrue, than to compare the French in France to the French outside, as though the first were the weak and the second the strong, the first submissive and the others brave. Before the war is over, there may be as many French deeds of courage and sacrifice accomplished under enemy rule as outside France under the free colors of the Allies.

There is also a danger of confusing the regime in France with the sentiments of the people living under that regime. France today is a prison, with two buildings. In one, the prisoners are guarded by Germans in uniform; in the other, the armistice has left an appearance of autonomy, and has set up a board of managers selected from among the French, although not elected by them.

The men in Vichy include, obviously, some sincere people, some confirmed and complacent defeatists, and some scalawags who sold out to the enemy. Frenchmen who work under the Vichy system belong in different categories as regards courage, capacity, and patriotism. But no matter who they are and what they wish, leaders and servants, they are prisoners like the rest.

Vichy is but a name for a temporary arrangement which suits some and makes others indignant. But behind the Vichy regime there is a Wiesbaden regime, a result of the conditions of the June 1940 armistice. The men in Vichy may plead, but not negotiate. They can beg or discuss, but they cannot decide. The really important decisions come from Wiesbaden and from Berlin.

A man can show infinite dignity in prison, and most French people do. What is *not* honorable is for a prisoner to proclaim his satisfaction in being rid, at last, of that burden called freedom. That, only a few Frenchmen have done. And these few will not count for much in the future of France, whether they stay in the lower ranks of the victor's services or disappear from the picture on the eve of an Allied victory.

What must be understood is that whereas Vichy rules over one third of France, it does not *represent* it. That it is a provisional makeshift falling somewhere between enemy occupation and real autonomy should be admitted more frankly. Slavery following defeat deserves a great deal of pity and understanding. But people who are fond of the simple truth do not like slavery which poses as independence.

It was thought necessary to write this brief comment about the Free French in order to state once more that this is a cause which deserves to remain always above the morass of politics, above ambitions and rivalries.

It should not be considered as a minority movement but as the expression of the real wishes and hopes of the French as a whole. Therefore, dealing with the Free French means dealing with that France which is real and will be lasting.

It is important for the American people to realize this, lest they ignore what sooner or later will become a valuable element in their own foreign policy. They should know that the rp 17 - irredentism